Schoolmastery

Schoolmastery

NOTES ON TEACHING
AND LEARNING

Donald Wilcox Thomas

To order additional copies of this book, contact:
Xlibris Corporation
1-888-795-4274
www.Xlibris.com
Orders@Xlibris.com
34528

Contents

THE PROFESSION

THE SCHOOL

DEDICATION

This book is dedicated to all teachers everywhere,
most especially to those with whom I have had the
privilege to work, and in particular to my daughter
Julia, who continues the family tradition,
and to the late George Bennett, my very
first mentor and my lasting inspiration.

Donald Wilcox Thomas

Preface

T he articles here collected span several decades. Some few have been published in journals and magazines, and several in a publication entitled *Reflections*, sponsored by and circulated within the Brookline Public Schools. *Reflections* "offered Brookline teachers and staff an opportunity to publish articles of interest to their colleagues and interested members of the community." As such it stands as a model that has encouraged innovative thinking among its readers and writers. Articles appearing under the heading of "The Memo" were prepared for a weekly memo circulated among the English department at Brookline High School. Besides messages regarding the daily routine, The Memo was intended to foster discussion and thought among the English staff. Over the years it became more widely circulated both within and outside the High School. Articles included herein constitute a selection. Unless otherwise indicated, the remaining articles have not hitherto been published. I am indebted to those publications that have permitted the reprinting of my articles in this collection.

Donald Wilcox Thomas
Bedford, Massachusetts, 2006

Introduction

S ignificant change usually comes about not by introduction of something new but by reinterpretation of something old. Among the more interesting illustrations of this premise is that of Arthur C. Clarke, who in *2001: A Space Odyssey* uses it to account for no less than the evolution of man. Back eons of time, so the story goes, herbivorous man-apes roamed the parched savannas of Africa in search of food, a search that had brought them to the brink of extinction. Their miraculous transformation from man-apes to ape-men did not come about until they realized that they were slowly starving to death in the midst of plenty, that the grassy plain on which they search in vain for berries and fruit was overrun with succulent meat. Such meat was not so much beyond mankind's reach as it was beyond his imagination. To negotiate the necessary transition, the man-apes had to reinterpret their environment.

The history of education can also be viewed as a sustained series of reinterpretations, which, because they remain human, retain remnants of the man-apes' primeval flaw—a certain primordial rigidity of the imagination that renders us unable to grasp what lies immediately at hand because it fails to correspond with what comes habitually to mind.

When it comes time to characterize the educational environment of the past few decades, it will undoubtedly be remembered as an era of reform. Cries for reform in education are by no means new to schools, of course, but seldom are they the focus of such prolonged and concerted attention as they have lately received. Not since the days of Sputnik have we witnessed such massive concern about what was happening or not happening in the nation's classrooms. In the sixties the thrust of reform focussed on the teaching of science and mathematics and spawned a period of curricular innovation that carried us well through the seventies.

It was an exciting time to teach, a time filled with openness and optimism and plentiful support.

But with the publication of "A Nation at Risk" in 1983 by the National Commission on Excellence in Education, a new interpretation struck. Suddenly, it seemed, everything had gone wrong: the schools had somehow fallen derelict in their duty to prepare the nation's youth to meet the manifold challenges that awaited them. Schools had degenerated into "Shopping Malls," SAT scores had plummeted to new lows, teachers had descended to shocking levels of incompetence, and content had turned to jelly.

Subsequent reports by other foundations, commissions, and "blue ribbon" panels confirmed the assessment. "American schools are in trouble," said John Goodlad. "After years of shameful neglect," according to Ernest Boyer, "educators and politicians have taken the pulse of the public school and found it faint." Horace Smith—Ted Sizer's mythical English teacher—was forced to compromise, but "dares not express his bitterness to the visitor conducting a study of high schools, because he fears he will be portrayed as a whining hypocrite."

Today, with the No Child Left Behind act, schools are embroiled in the tribulations of "accountability," with high stakes testing roiling instruction that must teach to the test and urban communities that must struggle just to keep their schools open. Meanwhile, as vouchers swell enrollments in private schools, charter schools have begun to siphon off students and teachers from the public schools.

As a schoolmaster for the past forty-five years, I view these changes with trepidation. A little too close to Horace Smith for comfort, I am nonetheless in no mood to compromise. Although I do not doubt that I am biased, it doesn't seem to me that my students have changed significantly over the years, nor for that matter the fundamental problems of education across the decades. And while I am thankful that my country is worried about its teachers and its schools, my fear is that the picture emerging is seriously imbalanced.

Perhaps the most significant feature of the current reform effort has been the conspicuous absence of the teachers' voice. Whatever the studies and statistics purport to show, few outside schools know what it is like to live and work inside them day after day. I am impatient with metaphors and analogies—unconscious or contrived—that portray schools as bad copies of other institutions or models of the marketplace, be they medical, military, industrial, or entrepreneurial. If such comparisons help us to reinterpret our educational environment, they are worth considering as long as we understand that schools are unique institutions and do not mistake the comparison with what it purports to describe.

I have taught in private and public schools, prep school and charter school, inner city and suburbs, Africa and Eurasia. And so I come to these pages as an uninvited guest, innocent of any panacea or huge anodyne, but with the hope of revealing one man's view of not only what schools actually are, but also what they might become. Because I am a high school English teacher, my view will quite naturally be swayed by the issues that arise there, yet will, I believe, apply to all schools as well, for what we most require is a change of attitude, a wakening of imagination that will help us newly confront our predicament.

"Schoolmastery" does not purport to claim the mastery of schools but rather to portray the weft and wiles of the redoubtable schoolmaster or schoolmistress, as the case may be, who seek to weave together the patterns of learning. I have chosen essays rather than a seamless imposition of remedies because teachers do not have time to read whole texts at a sitting and neither want nor need to be told how schools must be run. They want ideas, shared experience. Those who are able to endure reading all the essays here will undoubtedly sense the presence of a personal style and certain strands of abiding and overlapping themes. But I have not attempted to set forth a comprehensive portrayal of schools and all their concerns. I have tried instead to inject some practical ideas that will provoke discussion. My strategy has been to present schools as I have known them in hopes of stumbling upon some clues of plenty that lie fallow in our midst.

THE CLASSROOM

The Torpedo's Touch[1]

"In this thoughtful essay Donald Thomas communicates his teaching philosophy through one of his first experiences as a teacher. The setting of his story is the Harvard-Newton summer training program back in 1961 when he was one of four interns assigned to a master teacher and to a single class. The master teacher set the curriculum and the interns were required to teach parts of it . . . "

Harvard Educational Review, May 1985

R obert Frost once compared education to bringing a load of hay to the barn. The teacher stands on top of the load and the student waits below, ready to receive neat little packets. Instead, the teacher dumps the whole load, shouting, "Look out! Here comes education."

Such a comparison would have been out of fashion when I was learning how to teach. In those days B.F. Skinner had reached the pinnacle of his influence and had persuaded us to divide instruction into neat little packets, each of which could be duly "reinforced." The timing of such reinforcement was thought to be critical—down to the second, lest for lack of swift praise the implanted learning become extinguished like so many sparks falling on cold ground. Our method left no room for wonder or perplexity, no place for wisdom or sudden insight, because learning had been acclaimed a science, and science abjured whatever smacked of mysticism or romance.

The first lesson I ever taught fell sadly short of the anticipated ideal. I had been assigned to teach that dark corner of American literature represented by Jonathan Edwards. Faced with the grim preachings of this dour cleric, I decided that his writing would have to be dramatized if it were to stick. The lesson began with a recent newspaper account of a man who had been killed at a crossing by a speeding train. What was now fact, I suggested, might well have been predestined all along; the man and the train aimed to collide at the appointed time, irrespective of their individual traits or wills. Knowing nothing of their futures, the railroad engineer and his victim were powerless to change the inevitable course of events. My seventh-graders took that possibility in stride, since it had already occurred to them on separate occasions. But they entertained serious doubts about their fate being irremediably prescribed.

The ground being prepared, I now moved to set the scene, drawing the blinds and asking my students to raise their desktops in simulation of high Puritan pews. Reversing my coat and setting a lectern atop the desk, I mounted to deliver in muted Edwardian tones the fire and brimstone of "Sinners in the Hands of an Angry God."

It was a stunning lesson, if I may say so, however flamboyant. When the sermon ended, the students sat gaping and transfixed in their pews. I closed the book, the bell rang, and we were jolted back into our accustomed routines. In my twenty some years of teaching, I do not think I have managed to surpass the impact of that first class. Unfortunately, my supervisors were not so well pleased. There had been no fewer than ten of them sitting at the back of the room, all scribbling madly, anxious to demonstrate their critical training so that they might be authorized to judge rather than to teach. No sooner had the class ended than the arduous critique began.

At first I was cool and confident, secure in the belief that my lesson had hit home. But they were relentless in their queries. What had been my objectives? What had the children learned? How did I propose to measure this learning objectively? Somewhat taken aback, I struggled to explain what had seemed to me self-evident. The students had experienced what it was like to be a Puritan, how ruthless and discomfiting the doctrine of predestination could be, how graphic and powerful Edwards was in describing their predicament. But all of this seemed to no avail, and as the minutes crept by, I began to think that Edwards' congregation had not been so badly off. Sensing my gradual retreat, my inquisitors grew more aggressive. What skills had the students employed and what had been my strategy for reinforcing them? Was I aware that I had used *slang*? They swept aside my halting responses and pressed me hard for answers. "But what did the students learn?" In desperation I cried, "I don't know what they learned, but they'll never forget it!" Their victory complete, they let me go.

Recollected in tranquility, the lesson still shines, though its luster has softened considerably over time. Since that day, one of the supervisors still remembers me only as "Jonathan Edwards." I see now that in many ways it was the kind of lesson that only a young teacher might try, valor seeming the better part of discretion, and theatrics the lesser part of precision. Today, it would not occur to me to leap upon a desk, and more's the pity, for in that impulse lay a certain logic that I have since come to appreciate. I shall call it "the torpedo's touch," in honor of its ancient progenitor, Plato.

It was in reading the "Meno" that I first discovered my vindication. There Meno accuses Socrates of casting spells over his adversaries, at once enchanting and bewitching their minds. "If I may venture to make a jest upon you, you seem to me both in your appearance and in your power over others to be very like the flat torpedo fish, who torpifies those who come near him and touch him, as you have now torpified me, I think." To which Socrates replies, "As to my being a torpedo, if the torpedo is torpid as well as the cause of torpidity in others, then indeed I am a torpedo, but not otherwise; for I perplex others, not because I am clear, but because I am utterly perplexed myself."

The fish he refers to is what we now call the electric ray, which has a pair of organs that can deliver enough voltage to stun its victims senseless. These days, of course, the word torpedo suggests far more lethal consequences, like blowing one's students out of the water. Moreover, there are those who take exception to Socrates' notorious method of inquiry, which in the hands of the less facile and perspicacious can induce the kind of perplexity that may be deemed destructive to young minds. Indeed, the public is inclined to view philosophers as those who purport to see perplexity for its own sake where others find only detachment.

In essence, however, Socrates contended that we are better off knowing our ignorance, that the worst kind of ignorance is that which ignores itself. To prove his point, he volunteers to teach one of Meno's young slaves certain geometrical principles. Following his first demonstration, this conversation ensues:

Socrates: If we have made him doubt, and given him the 'torpedo's shock,' have we done him any harm?

Meno. I think not.

Socrates: We have certainly, as would seem, assaulted him in some degree to the discovery of truth; and now he will wish to remedy his ignorance, but then he would have been ready to tell all the world again and again that the double space should have a double side.

Meno: True.

Socrates: But do you suppose that he would ever have enquired into or learned what he fancied that he knew, though he was really ignorant of it, until he had fallen into perplexity under the idea that he did not know, and had desired to know?

Meno: I think not, Socrates.

Socrates: Then he is better for the torpedo's touch?

Meno: I think so.

In teaching we are too often persuaded to be gentle, fearing that we shall damage our children if we immerse them in dissonance or perplexity. We accede to the argument that each successive generation faces increasing complexity in life and so deserves greater sympathy and support to cope with mounting difficulties that assault from every side—recession, divorce, pollution, addiction, nuclear holocaust. We may argue that the young need not be torpified, but on the contrary require clarity, structure, simplification, reward. In their struggle to patch together the shreds of their identities, they reach out to us for guidance that we dare not withhold.

But perhaps it is we who fear the perplexity and disorder that for them is already intrinsic to life. For my part, I do not believe them to be in any worse straits than my generation. Like us, they long to experience life in all its fullness and measure. They are anxious to engage us in conversation that is real, undiminished, dynamic. Weary of little packets, they want the load.

And so each time I enter class I bring with me some part of the abyss that I plan to reveal. We begin, as Socrates so often does, with pleasantries and talk of surface things. And as they negotiate these waters, splashing amiably about in specifics, I lie in wait for them, ready to deliver the torpedo's touch and pull them under as far as they can go. I want them to leave exhilarated yet perplexed by what they have considered, conscious that we have managed but a glimpse of the depths that surge below. To be educated is to know what depths await us underneath the surface of things, whatever those things may be. To shield our children from life's inevitable perplexities is to leave them at the mercy of their ignorance and to deny them the wonder that is the basis of everything we know.

Backside Embroidery

I n the library, department heads were asked to meet with the Assistant Superintendent for Funds and Facilities who would be explaining the new system for creating all future budgets. We found him accompanied by an expert consultant conversant with an innovative procedure called PPBS that we later learned stood for Program Planning and Budgeting System, The gist of his proposal ran something like this. To begin with, we would need to specify each one of our disciplinary objectives or outcomes. We were then asked to assign a percentage of our yearly budget to the achievement of these individual outcomes. In English, for example, if one of our outcomes were the learning of literary terms or the grammatical parts of speech, we would need to affix a dollar figure to how much each of these was costing the school system.

The consultant, avuncular and condescending, patiently responded to our incredulous queries about how and why this needed to be done. In previous years we had submitted figures for teacher and administrative salaries, textbooks, equipment and supplies, workshops, and the like. Why then was the school requiring us to state clearly and explicitly the various goals we were seeking, the implication being that without such objectification we could not justly claim to be educating our children. Unless we could specify our goals, we were told, we could not lay claim to having any, which would not sit well with the School Committee. All sorts of trite metaphors were invoked in the service of this belief; e.g., if on an extended trip we did not know our destination, chances of our successful arrival were nil. Similarly, just as building a house without an architectural plan was futile, so too was teaching a lesson without clearly envisioning its outcome. One naturally hesitates to confess living or teaching without discernible purposes, seemingly bereft of any expressed aims or goals. What *form* these purposes should take and by what *stages* they should progress, however, are questions that underlie all such decisions.

But our real objection regarding the imposition of this new requirement lay in having to attach a monetary figure to each of these envisioned goals. On the one hand, communities have a right to know what is being taught in their schools and how much this is costing. To ask how much the parts of speech are worth, however, or the understanding of Newton's third law of motion is to press economic considerations beyond the pale. Our question to the Assistant Superintendent and his consultant was therefore this: if they would specify the relation that exists or should exist between learning and money, we would be able to undertake their request more seriously.

I am happy to report that they were unable to answer this question satisfactorily and that as a consequence, although we pretended to go through the motions that first year, PPBS thereafter died an unrequited death. Withal, it represents only the extreme of an approach that is still pervasive in education, an approach adopted largely from business practices where Management by Objectives (MBO) enjoys continued application. Because objectives in business are unitary, namely to cut costs and increase profits, corporate management by objectives is not a soul searching inquiry, its quarry being money rather than young minds.

Transmuted into education, however, MBO translates less well. "At the end of the lesson," as every lesson plan intones at the outset, "the students will know such and such and will be able to do such and such." In having students read 'The Lottery'," for example, we might stipulate that they are to understand the use of irony in this story. Or we might wish to ensure that all students understand the theme of the story and be able to articulate it in their own words. Having stated the lesson objectives, the plan moves on to describe the procedures to be used in reaching the stated objectives. They will read and discuss the opening paragraph. They will divide into small groups to isolate the steps by which the lottery is conducted. They will report back the conclusions of their small group discussions to the class as a whole. And so forth. And finally, the lesson plan will detail how the teacher will determine that the objectives have in fact been reached; i.e., evidence that they have learned the stated objective and can perform some function to demonstrate this learning. This will be a kind of rubric for judging the success of the lesson.

No doubt this constitutes salubrious mental training for student teachers, forcing them to untangle the manifold strands of learning and to focus on the encompassed skills that they wish to incorporate. Seemingly logical and straightforward, the process is nonetheless fraught with difficulties, implicating the following underlying questions.

- Do students need to know what they are supposed to learn in order to be able to learn it?
- How can we know what students already know or do not know?
- How can knowledge be conveniently divided into readymade components that fit neatly within a single class period?
- Is there some privileged sequence into which such components of knowledge may be reliably distributed in order best to be learned?
- Is knowledge that can be so divided and manipulated *worth* learning?
- What is the relationship between knowing and doing; i.e., how do actions reveal either the degree or quality of thought?
- Are all elements of knowledge equally accessible to demonstration through concrete evidence?
- When and on what grounds does a repeated action become a "skill"?
- How can we know what to teach until we have taught it?
- What is the relationship between what is taught and what is learned; i.e., how are they linked and is this linkage in any way predetermined?
- What is the relationship between knowledge and understanding; i.e., is the latter a matter of discerning the meaning of the former?
- Are there occasions in which understanding can precede knowledge?
- Does a lesson presume that acquisition of knowledge or understanding proceeds at a set pace, thus enabling all children to learn it at once?
- For whom must concrete evidence of learning be documented and why?

The problem with having learning driven by objectives is that objectives tend to drive the lesson at the expense of whatever else may be happening in class, which is usually a lot. Mandated to state their envisioned outcomes, teachers will naturally be inclined to ignore unanticipated outcomes, overlooking what may otherwise emerge that is both of interest and importance. In my experience objectives are learned not first but *last* and must be allowed to emerge. Otherwise, they tend to be mistaken, trivial, or simply not worth pursuing. In literature lessons, for example, a common stated objective is to understand the "theme" of a story. But in actuality stories have no themes, only interpretations that teachers may wish to impose, perhaps at the expense of student interpretations.

In writing we commonly discover our true object at the end rather than the beginning of a paper. If the primary thrust of a lesson is therefore to confirm achievement of some original objective together with attendant evidence and reinforcement of learning, then presumably revision of that objective can only take place when the lesson has "failed," forcing teachers to reassess their goals. It is in the nature of learning to have no objective save perhaps change. Management by objectives in education thus amounts to being definite about something whose very nature and interest appears indefinite.

It seems to me that when applied to learning, management by objectives is counterintuitive, turning the normal process of thought on its head. In teaching we are generally cognizant of the clumps of material for which we are responsible. Teaching normally follows the rationale that we most often find in books that begins with a table of contents or in the introductions of essays, neither of which is formulated in terms of objectives. Units of study, as they are often termed in school curricula, are also designed to carve out portions of content and a series of activities anticipated in examination of this content. In the teaching of subjects whose content is hierarchical and more or less sequential in the course of its acquisition, such as learning a foreign language, some aspect of mathematics or science, isolating objectives along the way is probably inevitable; e.g., the use of the subjunctive, the Pythagorean theorem, or Newton's second law of motion. But to state the behavioral outcomes of a unit in the humanities before it is taught is to put the cart before the horse. Here units of study thrust together items of content that may or may not have any necessary connection save in the mind of the teacher who, having predetermined the outcome, must ultimately trample unanticipated connections that arise. In reading history, an essay or novel, students need to grapple with the material on their own, not be told what they must learn, what causes or themes others may have extracted.

A wise and elderly neighbor of mine once observed that raising children is like working at the back of embroidery. On the front you see the colors and the patterns clearly, the design having reached a finished and orderly aspect. In back, however, the colors are all reversed, the patterns blurred, and the threads knotted, cut, and hanging loose. Parents see in their children all their history and their foibles, all the bad habits and loose ends. Outside observers stand at the front and see only the surface traits, thus often astonishing parents with good opinions of their children.

Teaching is like working at the back of an embroidery whose front displays order and design with distinct patterns but from whose back hang all the reverse colors and loose strands that teachers must manipulate in order to produce the unseen effect on the other side. It has been said that managers do things right while leaders do the right thing. Teachers must do the right thing by respecting the minds of their students who need to formulate their own objectives, discovering the power of their own minds. When students read a story, or consider a series of events in history, they should be made to grapple with its meaning for themselves, not wait for and adhere to someone else's interpretation. They have to see both sides of the embroidery and learn to work at its back where true learning resides, not mistaking the public face of learning for learning itself.

Dredging the Implicit

I n education, as elsewhere, according to Alfred North Whitehead, the broad primrose path leads to a nasty place. It is a place radically infected with inert ideas; i.e., "ideas that are received into the mind without being utilized or tested or thrown into fresh combination." A certain quantity of these ideas can always be pumped into the mind of a class on the assumption that acquisition of such knowledge "sharpens the mind" for later use. But for Whitehead this assumption breaks "the golden rule of education."

> *The mind is never passive; it is a perpetual activity, delicate, receptive, responsive to stimulus. You cannot postpone its life until you have sharpened it. Whatever interest attaches to your subject-matter must be evoked here and now; whatever powers you are strengthening in the pupil must be exercised here and now; whatever possibilities of mental life your teaching should impart, must be exhibited here and now. That is the golden rule of education, and a very difficult rule to follow.*

In schools the primrose path is paved with talk. The "nasty place" that awaits us is where, chalk in hand, we end up talking to ourselves. So bent are we on achieving our explicit goals that we reach them in spite of our students who sit passively before us waiting to be told what to learn.

Learning cannot be told because it is never explicit. That is the quintessence of the golden rule. So often we are tempted to say to students something like, "I taught it, but you didn't learn it," or "We went over that in class," meaning that we have talked about it and therefore all students need to do is pay attention to what we say and they will learn. But what do we say to the student who comes up to us and asks, "How do I get an 'A' on this paper or that test?" On the one hand, it seems a perfectly legitimate question. Since teachers do not award grades arbitrarily, there must be a reason or set of criteria that determines why some students get A's and others get B's and C's. The student is asking for the criteria. On the other hand, it does not occur to such students that if a teacher could actually tell them how to excel, there would no point in assigning grades. They probably believe that we can't tell them the answer without "giving it all away," thus spoiling our opportunity to make them "think."

Whatever we tell them, the real answer is that learning is always implicit, not a discrete list of things that can be written on the board or said in so many words. Take one of the most common lessons we learn in school—reading. Once we learn to decode letters—itself a very perplexing task—we move on to consider something called "The Main Idea." Teachers always want to know what The Main Idea is in what we read. When they ask what a story or essay is "about," they don't want to know what the words say; they want to know what they don't say. In order to discover this, we must "read between the lines." This causes students to wonder why, if The Main Idea is so terribly important, authors don't come right out and say what it is instead of beating around the bush. But they never do. Moreover, the more "important" the author, the more difficult The Main Idea is to find. It's another kind of game where the teacher ostensibly knows the answer, but the students have to guess what it is. Yet once the teacher explains it, The Main Idea always seems self-evident, thus giving students cause to wonder what prevented them from seeing it in the first place.

When we search for the main idea, solve a problem in algebra, look for cause of the Civil War, we dredge the implicit, examining new instances of patterns or events that remind us of something we know. Because we see only the products of our thought, its processes are inaccessible to us and therefore not subject to our deliberate control. We must dredge the implicit to find significance, scouring the surface of things for indications of what lies beneath.

When we walk into class, it is the implicit we must have in mind. It is something we see in the materials we shall consider, something that will be invisible to more inexperienced eyes because they do not expect to learn anything from something they think they already know. Yet in an important sense we can learn only by means of what we know. As Plato said, all learning is by recollection. Too often we teach as if all learning were by collection.

Instead of goals and objectives, I usually come to class with a question ranging in my mind. It is the kind of question that for students will not appear worth asking because it will already seem to have an answer. My task will be to ready students to consider this question and if possible, get them to ask it. Method chiefly consists of finding the right way and the right time to reveal the question. Since this timing will depend on student response, it cannot be precisely determined, but I estimate that it will emerge somewhere in the last twenty minutes when I want the discussion to peak.

To some extent, the success of the lesson will depend on my ability to predict what students will say and how they will react. I know, for example, that they will be most comfortable playing around with some of the specifics that I will initially provide them through the material. The lesson will have to be structured so that its importance is slow to dawn on them. They will need some time to reject the question as their initial response, or at least to discover large differences of opinion. If things work out right, the importance of the question will sneak up on them, so that they carry the lesson home. And finally, if I have taught the lesson before, I will know some of the things they will say and will have a couple of diversions ready that will momentarily relieve the pressure, allowing them to catch their breath before we plunge deeper. I want them to emerge *puzzled,* not perfectly clear, so that their conversation may continue over lunch and perhaps even dinner. Successful instruction ends up at the dinner table.

That is all I know about the lesson. I don't know exactly how it will begin or end, nor what they or I shall find to say. To that extent, the lesson will depend on their mood, which I will try to assess as I walk into class and go through the ritual of taking attendance. If they are noisy, I will give them some time to settle. If they are quiet, then I will begin quietly. If they look sleepy, I will accelerate the timing. Meanwhile, I shall rely on my foils to keep me apprised of where we are. Foils are students who habitually say whatever is on their minds, regardless of the consequences.

As a concrete example, let us consider one of Wittgenstein's language games taken from his *Philosophical Investigations.* The essential requirement for playing these games is the ability to ask questions. As students gain experience with the games, the tenor and thrust of their questions changes dramatically. At first, they naturally want to know the purpose and the rules for playing. Instead of providing them with an elaborate rationale and a list of rules, however, I encourage them to consider the content of the games so that in a formal paper they can ultimately decide the answers for themselves. Their assignment will be to define language games (I never do), to discuss in detail one of the nine games used in class (only two are Wittgenstein's), and finally to construct a language game of their own.

Here is the first game they receive.

LANGUAGE #1

> *Now think of the following use of language. I send someone shopping. I give him a slip marked "five red apples." He takes the slip to the shopkeeper, who opens the drawer marked "apples"; then he looks up the word "red" in the table and finds a color sample opposite it; then he says the series of cardinal numbers—I assume that he knows them by heart—up to the word "five" and for each number he takes an apple of the same color as the sample out of the drawer.*

> *It is in this and similar ways that one operates with words.*

I read the game aloud, slowly and gravely, then sit back and wait. After registering their initial shock—"This isn't a game!" "This is stupid!" "How can you play something like this?"—more substantive questions arise: "What's a cardinal number?" "Why does the shopkeeper go through all these crazy routines?" "What kind of table is he using?" "What has all this got to do with the way words are used?" At this point someone usually notices that, as the last sentence indicates, the game in question appears to represent the way our minds work when we use words, and that therefore it is probably a model or analogy for thinking.

Once this observation has been made, everyone readily agrees that this must be "the answer" and asks to move on to the next game. Short of any objection, this is precisely what we do, but usually there will be at least one student who will not accept so facile an answer, and who believes that thinking cannot be equated with shuffling charts, opening drawers, or mentally fingering words like a child learning to count. Invariably an argument ensues in which all sorts of other questions arise; e.g., if we don't carry swatches of red in our heads and if we cannot conjure up colors in our minds at will, then how do we manage to recognize, much less learn, the color red? We try to "see" colors in our "mind's eye" as they are called out with our eyes shut tight. Some will swear that they can see red or green or blue when their eyes are closed, that they dream in Technicolor; others insist they cannot.

It is often here that "the hoary question of other minds" can be introduced, which in this particular instance is the question I want them to consider. How, for example, can we know that what we see as red may not in fact appear green to somebody else who may have simply learned to call it "red"? For the time being, this notion will need some airing to see why it works, but because it will surface again later on, I do not press it.

Still, this is only the beginning, for a student may ask (as one actually did), "Why does the shopkeeper act upon the meaning of 'five red apples' in reverse order?" That is, instead of first counting to five, then looking up red on the color chart, and finally opening the drawer marked "apples," he does just the opposite. This raises the question of how we think about words—whether we process them in their given order as they are said or whether we think first of the noun (apples) before we process its modifiers (five and red). In turn, this kind of inquiry often brings up the question about the different functions of words, for although grammatically both red and five are modifiers, they nonetheless reveal unexpected differences when we look closely at how they are used. Red, for example, does not represent anything other than itself, since it has no existence apart from the substance it colors. "Five," on the other hand, represents an integral part of the number system and can never be part of any substance or thing.

Further still, when we say "five red apples" we mean that the last apple counted was five, not that five is the name of the fifth apple in the same way that red is the name for the color of that apple. Nor are there different kinds of five as there are different kinds of red. Even so, five can be represented in a number of different ways ("five," "5," "V," "11111." or a hand depicting five fingers); whereas, red can only be represented by a color of our own choosing—that is, not by magenta, crimson, maroon, etc. As for apples, we begin to wonder how only one name can comprehend so many different shapes, sizes, colors, and tastes, yet still remain just "apples." We note, too, that although "apple" can shift its role from a thing to a quality (as in "applesauce." "apple pie," "apple picking"), red and five make very awkward nouns at best.

These, then, are the kinds of questions that can come up in a single language game, though seldom in the fullness and depth illustrated here. What is remarkable, however, is how much of importance students can extract from what at first appears to be a silly little paragraph, how long they can spend doing it, and with what enthusiasm. What do these students say about this kind of learning? Here is what one student said.

> These are not games to play with other people but with oneself. The objective: to outwit one's own ability to overlook the most basic elements of human interaction, to brush aside one's life-long assumptions. In playing, one challenges himself, toying with the intellectual puzzle of human communication, and daring himself to speculate about the basic operations that occur behind the scenes.

In Medias Res

Why is it that, if we see a man stretching out his hand or his foot or anything of the kind, we do not do the same thing in sympathy, but if we see him yawn, we yawn in sympathy?

Why is it easier to hear inside a house from the outside than outside from the inside?

Why do hairs grow from scars on horses and asses but not on men?

Why do we smell burning spices less when we are near them?

Why does cold water make a shriller sound than hot when poured out of the same vessel?

Why do neither beasts of burden nor oxen nor any horned animal nor birds belch?

These are not the questions of a child but of Aristotle who filled two whole volumes with similar queries. Better known today for his answers than for his questions, he nevertheless observed that "the kinds of questions we ask are as many as the kinds of things which we know." Given the kinds of questions we find in his two volumes of *Problems*, of which the above are but a sampling, we sense a different person than we find in the *Politics* or *Poetics*. And yet we see here the workings of an acute and inquisitive mind that evidently took nothing for granted.

Aristotle also offered a few answers about questions. "It is clear," he said, "that all questions are a search for a middle." By middle he meant essentially a chain of implicit connections. Says he, "Call that term middle which is itself contained in another and contains another in itself." Then, in typical Aristotelian fashion, he proceeds to itemize four classes of questions:

(1)   whether the connection of an attribute with a thing is a fact,
(3)   what is the reason of the connection,
(3)   whether a thing exists,
(4)   what is the nature of the thing?

This being the sum and substance of his disquisition on questions, we may safely conclude that, for once, he had more to ask than he had to say.

The same may be said of children, whose mental life, like that of mankind itself, begins in earnest when they ask their first question. The most inquisitive creatures on earth, their questions would fill more than two volumes. Such relentless questioning indicates not only awareness that their understanding is incomplete, but also a belief that others who do not share their deficiency are willing to provide the necessary information. Armed with insatiable curiosity and a natural inclination to learn, the young child "values knowledge above all else." according to Chukovsky, and is "the hardest mental toiler on our planet." (*From Two to Five*)

But when they reach school at the age of five or six this natural process of learning is subverted, for here it is the teacher who asks the questions and the students who answer them. Schoolteachers do not ask questions because they are deficient in the knowledge they seek, nor because they expect their students to provide them with the information they lack. Quite the contrary: the purpose of questions in school is to determine if the students know or understand what the teacher already has in mind.

Once we have been subjected to interrogation in school, questions never quite regain their original intent, for we learn to value answers as indices of knowledge. Rather than ask what we truly want to know, we learn to circumvent our ignorance to avoid exposing ourselves to potential ridicule. Better to remain passive and appear knowledgeable than to risk discovery. Perhaps some other fool will ask what we want to know, thus gaining the desired information for us without jeopardy to our egos. We convince ourselves that the object of school is to find out what teachers "want" so that we can oblige them and move on to our next glorious stage in life.

Many students never fully recover from this sudden transition. All who have attended school vividly recall times when their ignorance was laid bare before their peers. In particular we remember those teachers who through their probing questions were able to reveal the rents and patches in our scanty preparation. I also recall times when we staked our reputations on what we thought to be clever responses only to win envy or suffer ridicule at the hands of the less venturesome.

How odd it is that education should be so conducted as to encourage this result. Were schools patterned after our more natural inclinations, we might witness classes in which teachers were mercilessly grilled by their students until the subjects were dispatched. Upon hearing what the students wished to know, the teachers would have to prepare their lessons accordingly. Once the class could ask more questions than their current teacher could answer, the students would move on to the next level of inquiry. The measure of a good teacher would then reside in how long he or she could keep a class at bay, while the sign of a good class would be how quickly it could expend a teacher's knowledge.

As things now stand, we come to appreciate the value of questions comparatively late in our education, if at all. We discover that the greatest leaps in knowledge arise from very simple questions—Socrates with the truth, Newton with the apple, Darwin with his finches, Einstein with capillary action, Piaget with chronic mistakes on IQ tests. Grounded in uncertainty, great questions begin by suspecting that things are other than what they seem and by sensing the inadequacy of received knowledge. Ultimately we learn that the capacity to frame a penetrating question ranks above that of answering such a question, for besides a fund of answers, a good question will also provoke a string of further questions; whereas, an answer speaks only for itself.

"But the mere putting of a proposition into the interrogative form does not stimulate the mind to any struggle after belief." cautioned Peirce: "There must be a real and living doubt, and without this all discussion is idle." Classes in which the teacher is the sole questioner and the students sole respondents do not induce struggle after beliefs, since in seizing all of the initiative the teacher leaves no room for doubt, real or living, save about what he or she may be thinking. Such "discussions" are idle because, however elegant or noble their end, they seek to rediscover thought rather than to provoke it.

If we would have students think, then we must allow them to pursue their own doubts and encourage them to rely on their own thoughts. More than this, however, we must teach them how to ask good questions, since "the way a question is asked," according to Langer, "limits and disposes the ways in which any answer to it—right or wrong—may be given." (*Philosophy in a New Key*) A good question must tell us what it wants to know. Moreover, a good question must be a *real* question: that is, it must be directed at something one truly wants to know, as opposed to a *school* question that asks about something that the questioner already knows.

To stress the importance of questions and to give students an opportunity to shape their own questions, we can employ a relatively simple technique that I call "Scattergroups," derived from the literal meaning of discuss, which is "to shake asunder or scatter." A scattergroup is a small group of people who come together to ask a question about a given topic and who then try to answer this question. Like all small groups, the scattergroup is designed to reduce the size of the audience so that those who tend to remain silent in full class discussions have a better chance to talk. Likewise, scattergroups are intended to teach students how to cooperate in a discussion. The crucial difference between a regular small group and a scattergroup is that the latter focuses on questions that students themselves generate. This process is divided into six steps.

ASK   Each member submits a question for consideration by the group and comments on every question submitted.

DECIDE   Under direction of a group leader, the group decides which question it will discuss.

SHAPE   Everyone tries to understand the thrust and scope of the selected question before attempting to find an answer.

ANSWER   The group tries to formulate an answer to its question.

SUM UP   Everyone helps pull together the main points of the discussion so far.

CRITIQUE Each individual draws his or her own conclusions about the conduct of the group's discussion.

Let us briefly examine each of these steps in turn.

Asking the Question: Scattergroups work best when students have been given some time to formulate their questions as concisely as they can, usually as part of an assignment. The purpose of this first step is have students hear, record, and comment on questions that all the other members have asked. In commenting on each other's questions, no attempt should be made to *answer* them, but rather to make sure that everybody understands what is being asked. This allows the questioner a chance to see the range of potential responses and to grasp the implications of what has been asked. Perhaps the question is ambiguous, thus increasing the range of plausible responses. Possibly, too much is being asked to provide a useful answer so that the question needs to be narrowed in order to produce an answer that will satisfy the questioner. But in no case should a question be dismissed. The aim of the group is to help every member ask a good question.

Deciding the Question: When everyone in the group has had the chance to explain his or her question, the group proceeds to decide which question they want to discuss. Sometimes several questions will converge on a common concern. Other times, one question will stand out above the rest. And at still other times, it will be necessary for the group to fashion a new question that somehow combines yet focuses those already asked. In any event they will need to have some criteria for deciding the question, and I provide them with the following guidelines which we discuss in class before they begin.

- A good question is a real question; i.e., it is directed at something one truly wants to know.

- A good question cannot be answered directly and completely. Questions eliciting factual information need not be discussed.

- Questions that seek to learn a purpose can be asked about nearly anything but can produce only speculation.

- A good question cannot be answered by a simple "yes" or "no." Such questions elicit immediate opinions and split discussants into opposing sides.

- A good question is not leading or rhetorical; i.e., does not embed an answer in the phrasing of the question.

- A good question sufficiently specifies what it wants to know to direct the course of inquiry.

- A good question considers practicality: it does not ask what people are unlikely to know through experience or unable to determine through discussion.

- Good questions are seldom asked; they are shaped through patient revision of not-so-good questions.

- The only "stupid" question is the one that remains unasked.

Shaping the Question: Once the group has decided which question they wish to discuss, they set about "shaping" that question. To shape a question is to ready it for answering, to "shake it down" by deliberately distorting its diction and construction so that it ends up specifying exactly what it wants to know. Questioners need to see the implication of asking "why" as opposed to "what," or "what" as opposed to "how." They need to anticipate the kinds of answers that these words typically provide and to decide whether this is the kind of answer they are looking for. Thus, in shaping the question they determine the form that the answer will ultimately take, and they begin to see both the thrust and the range of the inquiry inherent in the way their question is being asked.

Answering the Question: When and if the group reaches this stage of the process, the answer will be suspected if not already known, and the group can concentrate on filling in the details. If there isn't time enough to answer the question, the group should be able to predict the kinds of information the answer will include and foresee what obstacles stand in the way of obtaining such informatin.

Summing Up: Regardless of how far the group progresses with its question, it creates a summary at the end of the period in which it restates the chief content of its discussion and the problems it incurred. Summaries provide an abstract of the content rather than a recapitulation of the procedures so that discussion can pick up where it left off should scattergroups be resumed.

Critique. Critiques of the discussion belong to the individuals in the group rather than to the group as a whole. Each member is responsible for criticizing the discussion. These criticisms will be only incidentally related to the content already summarized by the group. Their purpose is to say something about the *conduct* of the discussion. Individuals consider special strategies employed, disagreements encountered, and most important, their own roles as discussants. Besides revealing flaws in the conduct of the discussion, they also offer suggestions for improving subsequent scattergroup discussions.

Students find scattergroups initially puzzling for several reasons. For one thing, the teacher has been completely removed, leaving them to rely totally on their own resources. For another, they are unaccustomed to dealing with questions in such detail, in particular their own questions. Moreover, they are frustrated by the deliberate postponement of the answer in the scattergroup process and will keep trying to hurry the process. Finally, having spent so long pursuing answers, it takes time for them to learn how to admire questions. Once the emphasis has been shifted from answers to questions, they are momentarily set adrift, believing there is nothing of value to be learned. They will wait for the teacher to rush in and rescue them from the necessity of having to think for themselves. They will beg the teacher to decide which question they should consider, or to tell them what he or she really "wants." In other words, having been thrust *in medias res*, they will experience real and living doubt. With time and persistence, however, they will resume the struggle begun in their earliest years, and as they become reacquainted with the joys of inquiry and their own suppleness of mind, they will acquire a renewed taste for plunging unaided into the thick of things.

Ladder Through the Sky

"I have heard this ever since I can remember, and ever since I have taught," said Robert Frost: "the teacher must teach the pupil to think. I saw a teacher once going around in a great school and snapping pupils' heads with thumb and forefinger and saying 'Think.' That was when thinking was becoming the fashion. The fashion hasn't yet quite gone out."

Frost delivered these remarks in a talk given at Amherst College in the autumn of 1930. More than half a century since, thinking has once again become the fashion in education. High schools have taken to calling themselves "cognitive learning centers." and increasing emphasis is laid on "critical thinking," "higher order thinking skills," "problem solving," "strategic reasoning," and the like. Despite advances in understanding certain mechanisms of thought—left brain right brain functioning, multiple intelligences, chemo-neurological relationships, learning disabilities, artificial intelligence models—we have not as yet managed to satisfy Frost's complaint.

Although we frown upon snapping students on the head with thumb and forefinger, we still ask them to think. However, we seldom tell them what thinking means. "To tell them," Frost said. "is to set their feet on the first rung of a ladder the top of which sticks through the sky." For him, thinking was "just putting this and that together . . . just saying one thing in terms of another." Essentially, he lived by metaphor and thought by metaphor. He believed that unless we were at home in metaphor, in saying one thing in terms of another, we were not safe anywhere, but particularly not safe in thought. Because so much of thinking is figurative, we must know how far it can carry us and just where our metaphors begin to break down. To speak of evolution, for example, is to liken the universe to a growing thing. Yet when we speak of the evolution of candy or of elevators we are exceeding the useful boundaries set up by the metaphor.

But if this is the first rung of Frost's ladder of thinking, then it is a very long ladder indeed or else its rungs are set exceedingly close together. To tell students that thinking is essentially metaphorical is not going to drop the scales from their eyes, nor even set their feet on that figurative first rung. As with all metaphors, we must know how far to carry it and where it begins to break down. We must understand for ourselves how thinking fits this mold, and if it does, how it may thereafter be applied.

My first clear memory of concerted thought harks back to a seventh grade social studies class. The teacher was a gentleman named Mr. Edgar. All I remember about him was that he wore glasses and beautiful cordovan shoes, was in his early thirties, and was friendly, shall we say, with my English teacher. But he was clearly frustrated with our class because we were pretty rambunctious and could be ruthless with his earnest attempts to teach us. The subject was geography and his question had something to do with why the earth did not continue to heat up and eventually burn from constant exposure to the sun, boiling the oceans dry. "Now before you try to answer this question," he said, "I want you to think very hard for a few moments."

Not really knowing what thinking was, I never knew exactly what to do when teachers asked me to think. So I resorted to replicating behaviors of people in evident quandaries. I remember holding my head in my hands and squeezing my eyes tight while inwardly repeating, "Think!" And then to my utter surprise it came to me, and before anyone else had volunteered I exploded with "I know!" Not being inordinately fond of me, no doubt for abundant reasons, Mr. Edgar uncharacteristically retorted, "I'll bet you don't know!" Somewhat taken aback by the energy of his reply (he obviously did not wish to waste a good question on me), I nevertheless delivered my answer—something having to do with radiational cooling. He was stunned, as were the rest of my classmates, since giving correct answers was an unfamiliar experience for me. "That's right!" he gasped, and I could see in his eyes that he was tabulating a quick reassessment of my dilatory mind. "That's very good!" he added generously, still absorbing the shock of having taught me something at last.

Mr. Edgar did teach me something, albeit inadvertently. He taught me that I could think. That I am able to recall this incident at all after so many years, much less with such clarity, confirms what a deep and lasting impression it made on me. I wish I could recount how this seminal experience transformed me into a model student, how from that very day I stuck my foot on the first rung and raced up the ladder, but that would be untrue. I continued in my dilatory ways for several more years until adolescence had been breached. Similarly, I wish that my experience could establish the broad applicability of some elegant method designed to teach "strategic reasoning," or "higher order thinking skills," which I could then confidently propound in the service of other recalcitrant students like myself. But the truth is that my awakening was probably fortuitous. All I did was put my head in my hands and close my eyes and the answer was there.

If there is a lesson to be derived, it is in part that thinking is much as Frost suggested, a matter of putting this and that together. Beyond this, it seems appropriate to me that all our great epic poets—Homer, Dante, Milton—should begin their works by invoking the Muse, which I construe as not dissimilar from holding one's head and closing one's eyes. The mistake of modern attempts to trap the Muse is the presumption that the process of reasoning, which amounts to thinking primped and scrubbed for public consumption, is itself reasonable. Current theory and research notwithstanding, we do not know enough about thinking to replicate it as a method or algorithm consisting of discrete steps or rungs in a ladder. This is not to say that we should ignore such theories or forego research. It is to say that we also need to examine our own experience as thinking beings and try to place it in perspective.

"It is the instincts, the sentiments, that make the substance of the soul," said Charles Sanders Peirce. "Cognition is only its surface, its locus of contact with what is external to it." That cognition is rooted in our whole being, but flowered at the surface of that being where we interact with the world, strikes me as remarkably apt. We think from our souls and with our hearts as well as through our minds. Thought is but the facing of our soul that reflects our inward sentiments and our outward gaze upon the world. It is the medium through which we assimilate reality and accommodate our natures. This is why something like poetry can strike a chord in us, because it addresses our feelings as well as our thoughts.

It is no accident that seeing is so closely allied with understanding. We do not have to be taught how to see. Vision is at once our most sophisticated sense and our most instinctive form of thought. In identifying a face we have seen before, we say that we re-cognize that peculiar configuration of flesh whose eyes and nose and mouth can otherwise assume infinite variety. This act of seeing is neither rational nor logical, yet it is among our most astounding feats of mind. When we do not understand what people say, we do not "see" what they mean in our mind's eye. Seeing is thus a primitive form of metaphor in which we put this and that together and behold a familiar face. To recognize something is to see one thing in terms of another; i.e., to grasp a particular image as a version of something we have looked at before.

I remember telling a student once that I do a lot of my thinking very early in the morning. I don't get up to think about anything in particular, I just let my mind run and see where it leads me. Often, I will teach a lesson, imagining myself in class. I become one of my students and listen to myself talk. If it doesn't sound right, then I back it up and run through it again, trying something different. Then I become myself again and have one of my students ask me a question or make a remark to which I will then formulate a reply. This can go on for an hour virtually without stirring. Similarly, just before class, I require a few minutes to myself. I am not thinking about anything in particular—usually just looking out the window, but something in my mind is settling and focusing.

Upon hearing all this, my student was stunned. For years he had secretly been doing the very same thing—secretly, because he was convinced that he was merely daydreaming when he should have been reasoning out some kind of problem or philosophy. I was the first adult he had ever heard confess to the same sort of mental dawdling—putting this and that together—yet identifying it as a legitimate form of thinking. I had given him license not only to think, but also to consider himself a thinker. He left my office standing on a higher rung.

If we had to teach children how to think, they would never learn. Fortunately, they come to us already equipped. Nor can we claim credit for teaching them to think merely by virtue of supplying them with things to think about. To treat the mind as if it were a muscle that bulges only when sufficiently exercised is to reside unsafely in metaphor. What we have to teach them about thinking is that each of them possesses this very special capacity that permeates their being, thus rendering them unique among all living creatures. They need to understand that this capacity is anchored in their sentiments and their souls, and that it stretches from there up through all the accomplishments of humankind, from art and music to language and literature, from history and culture to science and mathematics, from craft and sport to engineering and technology.

Above all, they need to see that thinking bears all the marks of humanity, that it is not wholly logical or obscure, lofty or precise, quick or sure. It is instead embedded in our dreams and fears from which it derives its true urgency.

Silence Reins

A s the old saying goes, speech is silvern but silence is golden. For Thomas Carlyle speech was not so much the art of concealing thought, as others of his day maintained, but "of quite stifling and suspending Thought, so that there is none to conceal." Silence, on the other hand, was "the element in which great things fashion themselves together; that at length they may emerge, full-formed and majestic into the daylight of life, which they are thenceforth to rule." (*Sartor Resartus, Book III*)

We would do well to consider Carlyle's assertion in the conduct of our daily instruction where not only talk, but primarily teacher talk, reigns supreme. Here silence is painful, an embarrassing lapse that, if allowed to continue unchecked, makes the students squirm until they slowly stiffen as an unnatural pall settles over the room, choking the lesson beyond retrieval. In silence we see only a void that desperately needs to be filled, irrespective of content. Being vacuous, silence is "boring," as our students are wont to say, whereas talk is filling, laden with learning. When our students say nothing, we can only assume that they are not "paying attention," that they are daydreaming, sullen, possibly distracted, and probably lazy because they are allowing their classmates to shoulder the responsibility for contributing to class.

Novice teachers quickly learn how strenuous it can be to talk pretty much non-stop for five hours each day and keep things moving. When lessons soar, hands shoot up, faces light up, and voices rise in volatile and overlapping talk. But when the pace is too slow and the pauses too pregnant, momentum is lost and students get either itchy or lethargic. One has to learn how to ask endless questions that will engage a class and elicit widespread response, how to orchestrate these responses so that every member of a class has the chance to contribute and feel a part of what is being discussed. Students want to know that what is being said is more than "just talk," that special meaning as well as information is being conveyed. More than talk, teaching is a kind of performance that gives voice to learning, a demonstration that becomes what it says, so that when the destination is reached, the students will know what has happened and be able to discern how far they have come.

> "To make oneself interesting artificially," says Maria Montessori, "that is, interesting to those who have no interest in us, is indeed a very difficult task; and to arrest the attention hour after hour, and year after year, not of one, but of a multitude of persons who have nothing in common with us, not even years, is indeed a superhuman undertaking. Yet this is the task of the teacher, or, as he would say, his 'art': to make this assembly of children whom he has reduced to immobility by discipline follow him with their minds, understand what he says, and learn; an internal action, which he cannot govern, as he governs the position of their bodies, but which he must win by making himself interesting, and by maintaining this interest." (*Spontaneous Activity in Education*, pp. 45-46)

We make ourselves interesting mainly by virtue of our talk, but this talk can also stifle and suspend thought. When he was visiting schools in Germany on an inspection tour in 1862, Leo Tolstoy recorded in full one such instance.

> Calm and confident, the professor is seated in the classroom; the instruments are ready; little tables with the letters, a book with the picture of a fish. The master looks at his pupils; he knows beforehand all they are to understand; he knows of what their souls consist, and various other things he has learned in the seminary. He opens the book and shows the fish. 'Dear children, what is this?' The poor children are delighted to see the fish, unless indeed they already know from other pupils with what sauce it is to be served up. In any case, they answer: 'It is a fish.' "No,' says the professor. 'Now what is it you do see?' The children are silent. It must not be forgotten that they are obliged to remain seated and quiet, each one in his place, and that they are not to move. 'Well, what do you see?' 'A book,' says the most stupid child in the class. Meanwhile the more intelligent children have been asking themselves over and over again what it is they do see; they feel they

cannot guess what the teacher wants, and that they will have to answer that this fish is not a fish, but something the name of which is unknown to them. 'Yes, yes,' says the master eagerly, 'very good indeed, a book. And what else?' The intelligent ones guess, and say joyfully and proudly: 'Letters.' 'No, no, not at all!' says the teacher, disappointed; 'you must think before you speak.' Again all the intelligent ones lapse into mournful silence; they do not even try to guess; they think of the teacher's spectacles, and wonder why he does not take them off instead of looking over the top of them: 'Come then; what is there in the book?' All are silent. 'Well, what is this thing?' 'A fish," says a bold spirit. 'Yes, a fish. But is it a live fish?' 'No, it is not alive.' 'Quite right. Then is it dead?' 'No' 'Right. Then what is this fish?' 'A picture.' 'Just so. Very good!' All the children repeat: 'It is a picture,' and they think that is all. Not at all. They have to say that it is a picture which represents a fish. By the same method the master induces the children to say that it is a picture which represents a fish. He imagines that he is exercising the reasoning faculties of his pupils, and it never seems to enter his head that if it is his duty to teach the children to say in these exact words, 'it is a book with a picture of a fish,' it would be much simpler to repeat this strange formula and make his pupils learn it by heart.' (Quoted in Montessori, Ibid, pp 47-48)

Here is the classic "guess what I'm thinking" lesson so familiar to all who have attended school. Although the content of the lesson is itself trivial, as Tolstoy makes abundantly clear, student interest derives from their desire to say something clever and their fear of saying something stupid. The teacher knows the answer but masks it through his questions. Like a riddle, the question is deliberately misleading, thus forcing the students to cast wildly about for the plausible answer that they think the teacher is seeking. Their interest has nothing to do with the object in question, merely in delivering the correct response and receiving the sparing praise and consequent good opinion of their misguided instructor. They know, too, that their most powerful weapon is the dreaded silence, in the face of which the teacher will provide them with a further clue, until ultimately the answer either becomes obvious or in desperation he is forced to reveal it. Students quickly learn that if they don't wish to play the guessing game, all they need to do is wait out the teacher.

The alternative to questioning students is simply to lecture them. The teacher talks and the students listen or take notes. Straightforward in approach, lecturing circumvents the problem of silence by filling all the available time. As Tolstoy suggests, lecturing is often the most efficient way to communicate a body of information: the teacher simply tells what he or she knows and the students "learn it by heart." In the early days of educational television, this was the favored method of presenting material. What you saw was a talking head, situated alone in what appeared to be a library. In a history lesson, for example, the talking head would quite literally *speak* history. Occasionally a leather bound volume would be plucked from the shelves behind and an appropriate reference read. The impression one gained was that knowing history enabled one to speak it, as if from memory, and that the speaker in question knew all the books so well that the correct volume could casually be located and the exact reference instantly found. Only later did we discover that these talking heads were actually reading from teleprompters, as our TV anchors do today, thus obviating their need to know anything.

In the question and answer approach, euphemistically termed "discussion," students sit silent and immobile until called upon. In lectures, students do not speak at all. While both approaches are goaded by the demand for constant talk, students remain largely mute, leaving them to muse, as in Tolstoy's recorded lesson, about such things as why teachers look over their spectacles instead of through them.

"In thy mean perplexities," says Carlyle, "do thou thyself but *hold thy tongue for one day*. On the morrow, how much clearer are thy purposes and duties."

We must learn to make the best use of silence. George Bennett, department chairman at Exeter, was a past master in the uses of silence. He would sit serene before a class contemplating a poem, saying not a word but musing by himself, perfectly at ease. He expected his students to think about what he had set before them and gave them time to do so. If he knew what the poem meant or what he wanted his students to think it meant, he never let on; nor did he intrude upon their thoughts with idle questions simply to fill the void. He merely sat and waited, patient and unperturbed.

Needless to say, for students unfamiliar with the rigors of silence, Mr. Bennett's equanimity was terrifying. Being left alone with their own thoughts for the first time in class, they found that they didn't have any, and would look at the teacher and then at each other in utter panic, seeking rescue from the mean perplexities of having to confront the poem unaided. But none was forthcoming. Mr. Bennett would merely look up and smile wistfully before retreating again into his thoughts. That was the first lesson: students were suddenly burdened with responsibility for their own learning, the focus of which lay before them, immersed in calm. There would be no riddles or clues, no interrogation, no forced revelations to escape the quiet. Their teacher stood aside, invulnerable to silence, allowing the poem to occupy the center.

At last some brave soul, preferring potential scorn to searing uncertainty, would speak, releasing the tension. Mr. Bennett would faintly start, his eyebrows lifted quizzically, as if someone had interrupted his reading in the park, and smiling, would nod his approval of the question or remark, then furrow his brow in thought, dazzled by the prospect of contemplating a wholly new interpretation of the poem. More looks askance among students, who, now that the ice was broken, were anxious to begin their task in earnest. But thwarted by the same equanimity, they saw that this new game was not yet over, for their teacher made no move to take the helm and urge them to safety. Fearing themselves unable to recover from a second immersion, they worked to keep the original query or remark afloat, while the teacher evinced surprise and delight at their interest. He would speak only to ensure his understanding of what they said, but avoid editing or correcting their remarks. Threading their way along, they would gradually begin to take hold, becoming more involved in the text, and speaking as much to each other as to Mr. Bennett, who, though plainly interested in what they had to say, did not attempt to usurp their lead. And then, suddenly, the class was over. He would give an assignment and they would file out, still uncertain of what they had learned or he had taught, but happy to shed their concentration.

And that was the second lesson. He would not usurp their responsibility for learning, would not suddenly assert his authority merely to break silence. They were co-participants in a common adventure to which he was indelibly attached. Ever serene and gentle, he demonstrated true respect for his students. For their part, they came to view him not as an equal but in true awe as one who sufficiently admired his subject to let it emerge, full-formed and majestic. "Of all the considerable men I have known," observed Carlyle," and the most undiplomatic and unstrategic of these, forbore to babble of what they were creating or projecting." George Bennett was one of these.

Making the Grade[2]

During one of those instant conversations that occurs between classes, a colleague recently observed how much fun teaching would be if only we didn't have to assign grades. As an afterthought, she wistfully added that without grades students would probably not do what we asked of them. Such is the tension under which we work day by day, caring to teach only for the sake of learning but knowing that grades drive students to learn what we teach. It is a kind of double bind in which we find ourselves: wishing to be respected for our judgment, yet not wanting to be resented for its exercise. Ultimately, each of us must come to terms with this tension on our own, balancing compassion with demand to create a scale of standards that, while serving students, also preserves our principles.

Over the years, I have come to view grades as more an opportunity than an onus. They provide an opportunity not so much for exercising authority as for teaching judgment itself, which I account central to our mission. That mission, as I see it, is neither to preserve nor to impose standards, but to teach them so that students will internalize the virtues we hold dear.

One does not teach standards merely by applying them in hopes that students will induce their proper criteria. If it is our intent to have students learn the meaning of the standards we espouse, then they need to understand how we arrive at them. Such understanding amounts to more than assigning weights to sundry tasks and then having students perform the required arithmetic to derive the proper sum. More, too, it is than simply explaining how we determine the various weightings. Our problem is how to teach judgment short of exercising it.

This problem is partially resolved by keeping our purpose foremost in mind. If our purpose is to teach how to judge rather than merely how we judge, then we must strive to convey the essence of judgment rather than merely providing isolated instances of it. One cannot teach judgment solely by making judgments.

Besides knowing how we judge, students need to know how they judge. And, if judgment is our quarry, we also need to know how students judge, which means that they must be given the opportunity to do so on their own, quite apart from our judgments. After all, it is they who need the practice, as well as they to whom these grades must always belong. If, on the other hand, students take no part in their grading, responsibility for their grades resides totally with us. They are then ours to give and ours to defend, which gives rise to the anguish we suffer over grades.

You know the drill. We assign a "C" to a student who insists he deserves a "B." He declares that he has never received a "C" in this particular subject. The parent calls and says that there must be something wrong because she has read all her son's papers, as well as those of his friends, and thinks he deserves no less than a "B-." The student has stayed up nights typing papers, has done all the work, never been absent, and never worked so hard. In elementary school he got all "A's," but since coming to high school his writing has gotten worse instead of better. So we haul out our grade book and read off the grades, which, of course, only serves to beg the question because what the parent really wants is for her son to go to Harvard irrespective of his judgment or his grades.

Why do we worry about grades? Because we set ourselves up as the court of last resort where the evidence for crimes committed is usually circumstantial. We can be as mathematical as we like, but ours is at best an inexact science and at worst a matter of taste and opinion that is always subject to challenge. Grades have about as much substance as list prices. Everybody, it seems, wants a discount: discount the spelling, discount the syntax, discount the style, the originality, the coherence, the economy, and the judgment.

I never put a grade on a paper. I write comments instead, telling the student where the paper succeeds, where it falls short, how it might be improved. Because these comments take time to write, I want to ensure that the student reads every line, trying to translate my remarks into an overall judgment of the grade. My object is to have the student judge the paper in light of my remarks rather than taking issue with my grade. I want students to attend to their reading and writing. Grades on tests and quizzes I will give, but discussion of grades must wait till marking period.

That is what makes marking period an opportunity. I tell my students that I have only two criteria for grading. The first is that an "A" signifies sustained excellence and everything else is discounted proportionately. The second is that anyone who misses an assignment starts with a "C," since "B" signifies good work and those who have failed to complete work cannot be judged as doing well. I remind them that by its very nature a grade must be comparative; otherwise, it's meaningless. And since I am the only one who has seen everybody's work (and am not exactly new at this task), I am in the best position to judge comparative worth. They, on the other hand, are in the best position to judge themselves as individuals, since they are unique, and since I can never fully know them.

Ideally, then, a grade will be a composite of their judgment and mine. On the last day of the term, I ask them to fill out a card with the following information. First, I want them to comment on their work, telling me anything they want me to know. This is not an assessment of the class (which comes later), but an assessment of what they have done. Second, I want to know what their criteria are for judging a grade. I ask them to list them in order of their importance and to give themselves a grade for each criterion. Finally, I ask them to assign themselves a single grade that best represents their work. I admonish them not to play games with the grade but to be honest.

I then explain what I will do with these assessments. In my grade book, I will set aside columns with the following headings: Mark, Grade, Term, Conference, Change. Under "Mark," I will place their grade, under "Grade," my grade, and under "Term," a tentative composite of both. If we agree, then, of course, they get the grade they have chosen. If we don't agree, we will have a conference. If as a result of our talk, we decide that a change in the tentative grade is in order, then that will be recorded under "Change."

The essence of this procedure is the opportunity it provides for conversation, which I usually end up having with every student, so that we can share our opinions on papers and grades. My concern is whether they overestimate or underestimate themselves, since this helps me to anticipate how to handle our differences of opinion. In some instances, my own grade will be influenced by the student's assessment. But for the most part these grades seldom differ more than one third of a grade. When this is the case, I tell the class that I will be inclined to go along with their assessment because I don't really care whether they work to get a grade or work to keep it. If we differ a second time, however, then the grade must go my way. Most important, when they overestimate their grades, and we decide to accede to their opinion, they have registered my doubts and know they must now convince me about their judgment. Conversely, when they accept my opinion, they know that I have also registered theirs. If we disagree the first time and they go along with me, then, in the event of a second disagreement, it is understood that the grade will go their way. But it is also understood that I must retain ultimate responsibility for grading, and that I will not give any student a grade I don't think he or she deserves.

Although I hasten to affirm that not every student adores this process, I don't remember ever receiving a call from a parent about a grade. There could be several reasons for this, but I believe it is primarily because this approach leaves room for listening and for trust. Students don't complain about grades they think they deserve. It grants to students some say in what shall become permanent facts in their records. Best of all, without diminishing the importance of grades, it puts them in their proper place and allows us to get on with the business of learning.

Great White Elephant

D own the length of the corridor on any given day in the New York public school where my daughter teaches, she can hear exactly the same history lesson being taught in every classroom. Here "being on the same page" is taken quite literally, for it is a page drawn from the curriculum framework known as "The Regents," a regimen of required subject matter so compact that it leaves no time for divergence and little room for creativity. A longstanding system of centralized curriculum control, the Regents (named after the governing New York Board of Regents) bear more resemblance to European models than to public education elsewhere in America. This is why junketing foreign educators nearly always stop off in New York State to view schools that are most nearly like their own, and why those who come to Boston, where universal public education originated, are shocked to find educational policy determined locally by school committees in our cities and towns. At least, that's the way it used to be. To be sure, although neither system is perfect, the cost of disparity among local schools seems well worth the price of freedom that enables us to determine our own educational criteria.

Yet now, quite suddenly, in the name of education reform in Massachusetts, we find ourselves under the moving shadow of "accountability" in the form of "MCAS," the Massachusetts Comprehensive Assessment System. This series of tests has been mandated by the state to be administered each year to grades four, eight, and ten in English, math, science, history, and world language. By the year 2003 all students were required to pass the MCAS in order to graduate. Concomitantly, a series of curriculum frameworks has been published that spells out the subject matter that each test will cover in each of the three grades in which they are to be administered. Both the frameworks and the tests themselves have been conceived and written by select groups of

Massachusetts teachers drawn from all over the state and from all the respective disciplines.

Administered for the first time over a period of seventeen hours in the spring of 1998, the results of these initial tests, which we were told would "not count," were not released until the end of the year, having been corrected by a group of paid non-professionals over the summer months, then meticulously tabulated for release. To no one's surprise, as soon as numbers were attached to these results, they were instantly published in the press, the inevitable comparisons between and among schools summarily made, and inferences about the status of education throughout the state freely drawn. What we learned was that education appeared in pressing need of reform, such reform being most urgent in proportion to the diminished economic status of the students involved, suburban results far outstripping urban results.

That millions upon millions of dollars (some 50 in all) should be expended by so few to produce such unstartling results from so many does not account for the damage yet to be done by this great white elephant trampling amid our individual fields of inquiry. Questions abound.

To begin with, why go to all the trouble and expense of producing yet another series of standardized tests when we already have such tests available; e.g., the SAT's, Stanford 9's, and the ACT—tests created by professional test makers and boasting a national data base upon which to draw. With all due respect to my colleagues who volunteered their services in creating the MCAS, such tests are extremely difficult to design and construct so that they not only comprehend the full range of capabilities in question, but also prove challenging and interesting to all concerned, thus producing a fair assessment of student learning across the board. In the tenth-grade English test materials, for example, we initially found such authors as James Joyce, Virginia Woolf, Thomas Wolfe, Flannery O'Connor, Thomas Mann, and Joseph Conrad—clearly a luminous list of literati. Granted that criteria for choosing these authors may have sought those with whom sophomores were unlikely to be familiar, it would appear that my colleagues may have been more concerned with their own reputations than with the experience and abilities of average high school sophomores.

It is understood, of course, that tests must always be revised, especially brand new tests, which these most assuredly were. But consider that this is only the beginning, for besides the expense of hiring people to correct these massive tests each year, the tests themselves will have to be rewritten so as not to repeat what has gone before. Tabulate the high cost of producing, distributing, administering, collecting, correcting, publishing, and then revising these tests each year. Bear in mind that all the decisions being made rest not with professional monitors, but with a collection of local teachers. Add to this task, the whole framework of mandatory curriculum that is supposed to undergird these tests.

Quite apart from the questionable reliability of these tests, to say nothing of their validity, when was it ever a good idea to have a small group of teachers decide for all the rest of us what should be taught? Exactly when and why did teaching lose the capacity to decide this for itself? And what sort of teachers do we hope to attract who exercise no real say in either the content or assessment of their teaching? After all, one need know nothing about teaching, learning, or adolescence in order to mandate such tests. What we most need to know is *how to teach* whatever there is to learn, not what to teach or even when to teach it.

Questions nevertheless arise not only about the what of curriculum, but also about the when, for under the present arrangement high school teachers are given only a year and a half to teach the assigned subject matter; i.e., ninth and one half of tenth grade. Consequently, in matters of history and science, not only the substance of curriculum but also its sequence is being dictated. Is there some privileged time to teach world history as opposed to American history? Biology as opposed to chemistry? Algebra as opposed to geometry? And supposing students fail these tests; when and how do they make them up, given that the material covered may not be taught in subsequent grades? And why are we administering the MCAS in the 10th grade when it doesn't have to be passed until graduation? In other words, why are schools being given only two years instead of four in order to meet the MCAS standards?

Beyond the test takers and the test makers, what about testing itself? Let us not rehearse the litany of reasons for holding teaching accountable. Nobody teaching expects to avoid responsibility for what they teach and what their students learn. Let us look instead at what we are holding people accountable for. Leaving aside perhaps the most pressing issues that confront schools, namely, those of *race, class, culture, health, familial support, educational background, learning disabilities*—all of which MCAS testing discounts, the question that confronts us is what impact testing exercises on educational reform. Clearly, testing itself does nothing to increase student learning. The abiding premise therefore seems to be that if these tests produce the kinds of results everyone already expects, teachers and schools will be *frightened* into teaching students what they should know. It constitutes a version of the troglodytic approach to problem solving, namely, "if it doesn't work, force it." Purely as a matter of public humiliation, schools will get their acts together and stop fooling around. Teachers will teach to the test. Errant schools will be taken over, principals and teachers fired, military discipline enforced, uniforms donned, teaching focused on testing to the exclusion of other nonessential subjects—music, art, home economics, vocational training. And so, in ridding ourselves of "bad schools" we shall improve education of all schools.

Plainly enough, the MCAS tests are designed to pit schools against each other, to make education competitive, a watchword of capitalist entrepreneurs. Like unsuccessful companies, schools will simply be put out of business. It will be teach or die. As we have already seen in Boston, however, one result is that outlying communities begin to question the impact of importing urban students who are bused to the suburbs, fearing that their overall scores will unduly diminish, thus causing the more financially secure populations of professionals to seek housing elsewhere. Start talking real estate and suddenly education takes on a new urgency. Or, as has been the case in Boston, the number of dropouts will increase exponentially as well as the number of grade retentions.

What about alternatives to MCAS? Certainly in the present decade we have witnessed more innovative and humane approaches to assessment; e.g., the use of portfolios, exhibitions, juries, journals, and internships. In the mean time, a whole movement of charter schools has been launched to experiment with different modes of instruction employing alternative emphases on content and method. Yet now the parameters for investigation in charter schools have been drastically constrained by the demands of MCAS, the fear being that charters will not be renewed unless teachers adhere to published curriculum frameworks. So much for innovation! Like everyone else, charter school teachers have no choice but teaching to the test. Finally, as far as colleges are concerned, the SAT's and ACT tests shall remain the accepted standards for admission, not the MCAS, which can have no comparative value outside the state.

If decades of experience with New York's Regents exams had produced an education that was clearly superior to our own, that would be reason enough to try out their scheme. My daughter assures me that uniformity of teaching and testing is not the solution. Education reform has never worked from the top down. No doubt our enterprising commercial publishers are already hard at work producing textbooks that incorporate the new curriculum frameworks. Perhaps we shall once again be subjected to "teacher-proof" curriculum that last emerged (and died) in the sixties. But deep down we all know that schools can be no better than the people who make them—the students, the parents, and the teachers. They are a reflection of their constituents, which is all that the MCAS and similar tests in other states have been able to confirm. Meanwhile, ever since Proposition 2 1/2, which severely limited yearly increases in Massachusetts property taxes, we have also seen the gradual but systematic erosion of the curriculum to exclude art, music, theater, home economics, and sports, none of which are touched upon by MCAS. Similarly, school facilities continue to suffer from years of neglect.

Far from making teachers and schools accountable, the MCAS has effectively removed their accountability for creating, teaching, and assessing what students learn. If true education could be had simply by virtue of mandate, we might be the most learned nation in history. Conversely, our strength lies in our diversity and our individuality. That we do not cotton to such mandates is perhaps a better measure of our educational quality than any test.

Silver Cross Soft Amethyst[3]

E ducation waits upon the moment. Call it a moment of revelation, of recognition, of sudden enlightenment or clarity—what you will; it comes creeping on us unawares, often when we least expect it. When teachers speak fondly of children's eyes alight with learning, they speak of this moment towards which all instruction is ineluctably drawn, its design being to incite in pupils an instant when things fall together, stunning them into realization. It is the moment when the mist surrounding routine affairs briefly clears, enabling them to see plainly what is otherwise shrouded in detail. In this special moment things stand still just long enough for them to take hold and turn a piece of the world in their minds.

In advertisements for commercial materials we see depicted the smiling faces of children deliberately set aglow as a dramatization of these coveted events, as if use of the material in question were programmed to enkindle chronic states of enlightenment in its happy victims. No agony of thought creases their youthful brows, no struggle after belief slants or glazes their eyes as they are led through the minefields of learning. Education for such as these purports to be nothing less than a string of timely epiphanies cunningly contrived to punctuate their hour of instruction, like an endless ride through Disneyland where plastic alligators and stuffed jaguars lunge and hurtle at spectators at strategic intervals.

Teachers know better. It is the casual and inadvertent remark, the parenthetic observation, the personal recollection blurted out in momentary lapse from formality that sticks in the mind, and that, years hence, resurfaces in testimonials of ardent alumnae, much to the consternation of the teachers who have long since forgotten, and often cannot even remember thinking what they are told they said. I recall the story of one such teacher, ancient and venerable, who had at one time held sway in the teaching of physics. Approached by a grateful alumnus, he listened patiently as his former student heaped praise upon him for his memorable lessons concerning the specific heat of steam. So clear and forcible had his explanations been that it had lain untainted in the mind of his appreciative student for decades. Thanking his former student, the teacher asked, "By the way, what *is* the specific heat of steam?"

For me one such moment of epiphany lay dormant in a line of Keats's poem "The Eve of St. Agnes." Until this moment poetry had remained a hazardous and shiftless pursuit in which one feigned enthusiasm for a medium shrouded in mystery and rife with pedantic allusions, thatchy syntax, opaque images. Knowing poetry to be laden with deep-inner-hidden-universal-meaning, one resolutely poked and stabbed at it like boys upon a carcass until the teacher relented and delivered its shining message—Knowledge is Good, Love is Great, War is Hell.

So began "The Eve of St. Agnes":

> *St. Agnes' Eve—Ah, bitter chill it was!*
> *The owl, for all his feathers, was a-cold;*
> *The hare limp'd trembling through the frozen grass,*
> *And silent was the flock in wooly fold:*

Named for a martyred Roman virgin, we are told, St. Agnes' Eve fell on the night of January 20th when, in olden times (poetry was always about olden times), young girls could, upon ritual performance of certain rites, foresee in their dreams the visage of their future husband. Taking care not to look behind them, they would lie in bed, hands beneath their heads, and in their dreams their husbands would appear, kiss them, and then share a feast. How very quaint and touching a tale was this, thought I, though at the time I was not principally interested in girls' dreams, virginal or otherwise.

Notice the concrete imagery demonstrating the frigidity of the night, says the teacher: the owl despite his feathers was nonetheless cold; the hare for all his coat limped! Because this was the sort of game that excited English teachers, it was easy enough to guess at further instances of concrete imagery. One could wisely observe, for example, how even the sheep with all their wool were frozen still. So, too, for the numbness of the beadsman's fingers as he told his rosary, his frosted breath "taking flight for heaven." He was praying, you see, so his words, encased as they were in vapor, rose heavenward to their destination. Very nice. And then, of course, there were the knights and ladies praying who "ache in icy hoods and mails."

Cold! Really cold on that particular January eve. Only 372 more lines to go! Anon—line 54—comes Madeline.

> *Full of this whim was thoughtful Madeline:*
> *The music, yearning like a god in pain,*
> *She scarcely heard: her maiden eyes divine,*
> *Fix'd on the floor, saw many a sweeping train*
> *Pass by . . .*

Some music this that provokes divine pain, yet we see that it is actually the pain of anticipation in Madeline, who is anxious to get on with the evening—a psychological simile. The synecdoche of "sweeping train" is also dutifully noted. Then across the moors speeds young Porphyro (Porphyro? What kind of name is this?) "with heart on fire for Madeline."

Not until she reaches her boudoir do things start to pick up. Meanwhile, the wily and inflamed Porphyro is scheming below with the aged Angela on how to secure secret entry into Madeline's chamber—"silken, hushed, and chaste." My attention now focused, I marvel at this redoubtable lad who dares sneak into a girl's bedroom at night with neither her nor her parents knowing. Guts!

> *. . . her vespers done,*
> *Of all its wreathed pearls her hair she frees;*
> *Unclasps her warmed jewels one by one;*
> *Loosens her fragrant bodice; by degrees*
> *Her rich attire creeps rustling to her knees:*

Jesus—warmed jewels, fragrant bodice, rustling to her knees—this Keats can write, I see. But then, too, the arresting lines just before:

> *Full on this casement shone the wintry moon,*
> *And threw warm gules on Madeline's fair breast,*
> *As down she knelt for heaven's grace and boon;*
> *Rose-bloom fell on her hands, together prest,*
> *And on her silver cross soft amethyst,*
> *And on her hair a glory, like a saint:*
> *She seem'd a splendid angel, newly drest,*
> *Save wings, for heaven: Porphyro grew faint:*
> *She knelt, so pure a thing, so free from mortal taint.*

Beside Porphyro, I, too, am giddy, but now the teacher wants to analyze the lines, the color imagery. With me hooked in the amorous grip of the story, he wants to intercede with image analysis—so typical!—the rose-bloom on her hands, on her silver cross soft amethyst. . . . . Amethyst? Hold it a second. Where does he get the amethyst? Then I see it: Madeline kneeling in the moonlight and the light on her cross flashes amethyst. Exactly! Silver does that, though I had never noticed. Yet I must have noticed since I immediately saw it; I had just never noticed noticing it, never thought it worth noticing.

Keats had. And now I am suddenly, almost absurdly taken with this tiny detail. Here's this lovely creature set before me, kneeling in the moonlight, and on her cross soft amethyst. It was as if Keats and I were huddled together behind the arras in Madeline's silken chamber, and he leans over to whisper, "Ever notice how in certain soft lights silver gives off the hue of lavender, like amethyst?" Transfixed by the cross gleaming on her breast, I reply, "Yeah, as a matter of fact, I have noticed that."

Across the years right on the page I catch somebody seeing, some living being just like me who looks at things with a probing eye; who feels the cold in his bones and knows that sheep stand close to ward off the chill; who can imagine what it's like being an owl in winter or a rabbit hopping across frozen grass; who thinks about how mail armor must ache in icy cold and how bodies warm the jewels that grace them; who knows what young maidens dream and young lads hope; who knows that silver in the moonlight reflects soft amethyst. What's more, he knows not only what he thinks is beautiful, but also what I think is beautiful.

But how the devil can he know all this? This isn't the kind of stuff you learn in school, never mind the ornamental lines of Poesy. Or is it? It is and has been ever since. Truth is beauty, beauty truth. More than I expected to learn, it was, indeed, all I then needed to know.

THE MEMO

Where Curriculum Lies

O n occasion I get calls from people requesting copies of our curriculum. Usually they are from schools that are contemplating changes and want to know "what's out there." Although I am always curious to discover why they are calling me to gain this information, I never ask. Perhaps they have read *The Good High School* or Boyer's book, have met one of our staff at some far-flung conference, or simply know somebody who went or taught here.

In any case, responding to such queries is always a little difficult because I never know what they mean by "curriculum," a term they use as if it required no further explanation. This sets up a kind of double bind in which, while posing as a "Curriculum Coordinator" of evident repute, I am placed in the potentially awkward position of not appearing to know precisely what it is that I am coordinating. Asking for "curriculum" is not unlike walking into a restaurant and asking for "food." My strategy is therefore to present them with a kind of menu consisting of appetizers, entrée, side dishes, and desserts, as if we had more to offer than they could possibly consume. My immediate object is to intimidate them with the seeming magnitude of their request in the hope that I can persuade them to go *a la carte* and tell me exactly what they want.

In some instances this works quite well, since we are able to discover that, rather than the main course, all they want is a side order of "grammar," "the writing process," "multicultural literature," "female authors," "interdisciplinary topics," "advanced placement," "heterogeneous grouping," and so forth. In these instances it becomes clear that instead of renovating they are busy patching holes in their offerings, making them presentable under the fleeting glare of fashion.

In other instances, however, we learn that they are simply casting about in the fond hope of finding some exotic dish with which to season and garnish their own menus. They are looking for something they know not of, something at once intriguing yet sound. This is a more difficult query to satisfy, though not impossible. There is always semiotics, laptops, literary journalism, the aids seminar, the mind's eye, autobiography, the senior paper, what have you. I feel like the proprietor of a curriculum boutique, offering designer specialties to the uninitiated. Oddly enough, if I can't sell something we do, I get trapped into feeling absurdly inadequate, even though it is we who own the merchandise and they who come to fill some indeterminate need.

The real oddity of these periodic exchanges, however, is the underlying belief that teaching can be transferred, packaged, and shipped from one environment to another. I am invariably disappointed to discover how little people actually want to know, and consequently how paltry is the common conception of curriculum. They manifest endless gratitude for receiving little packets—catalogue descriptions, syllabi, reading lists. Perhaps they are only being polite, not wishing to trouble me. Possibly they are conducting a cursory or reluctant investigation, already convinced that what they are doing is right, but going through the motions just to confirm their suspicions. After all, is not English a common discipline, universally taught in schools throughout the country, and do not teachers of English therefore share a common bond?

Not really, although what passes for curriculum leads us to believe otherwise. Ostensibly, we teach reading and writing, speaking and listening, viewing and thinking. We divide our literature into American, British, European, and world. Like others, we have inexhaustible lists of skills that our students are supposed to acquire. Yet to my mind this cannot begin to encompass what we do.

Curriculum is not what we do. Nor is it what students do. Curriculum is what we think about what we do. Students do not learn curriculum; they learn what we teach them. What need have we, then, for curriculum? Answer: to learn what we think about our teaching. And what determines what we think? Although this question deserves detailed analysis, for now the answer must be "nearly everything."

Were I therefore an honest and forthright man, a true coordinator of curriculum, I would have to be no less than a wizard, privy to the innermost thoughts of my teachers, not to mention thoughts of my own. I would have to be a Doctor Frankenstein capable not only of penetrating but also replicating thought and experience. In that dubious role, this is how I would then respond to inquiries about curriculum. I would clone teacher brains, bottle and ship out chunks of cortex in regular installments to be surgically grafted onto willing minds, since it is here that curriculum truly resides.

Teaching Curriculum

"To write a work of genius," said Virginia Woolf, "is almost always a feat of prodigious difficulty. Everything is against the likelihood that it will come from the writer's mind whole and entire. Dogs will bark; people will interrupt; money must be made; health will break down. Further, accentuating all these difficulties and making them harder to bear is the world's notorious indifference . . . If anything comes through in spite of all this, it is a miracle, and probably no book is born entire and uncoupled as it was conceived."

M ight not something similar be said of teaching? Fraught as it also is with difficulty, seldom does it achieve our full intent. Prepare it as we may in private, we do not have the luxury of perfecting and delivering it whole, straight from our deliberations. And though like writing our medium be language, we exercise only marginal control over the circumstances that comprise its context. We must teach not only those who know less than we, but also those who may not be anxious to hear what we have to say. Unlike that of the author, ours is a captive audience that while seldom indifferent can easily be distracted and on occasion disruptive. And yet, in spite of all this, the miracle of teaching regularly occurs, howsoever crippled in our conception.

But the most pronounced difference between writing and teaching is that, albeit rare and fleeting, our genius stands unrecorded. Great writing is by definition that from which all may learn; once written it remains fixed for generations of readers to take from it what it encompasses, even to derive lessons that may not originally have been intended. Teaching, on the other hand, is a one-night stand that can never fully be replicated. It is a performance whose performers age with each presentation, whose expertise increases with each trial, but whose execution is subject to the vicissitudes of circumstance. Great teaching lives in the taught but dies with the teacher.

In education we have no works of genius. We have only curriculum. It has been the fallacy of the past to equate teaching with curriculum as if the two were interchangeable. In the classic lesson plan we ask teachers to state their intent by enumerating their goals. We wish them to know how they propose to achieve these goals, in what activities the students will engage to attain the specified enlightenment. And finally, we want to know how the teacher plans to secure this enlightenment so that what has been learned may be not only demonstrated but also applied.

At the heart of every lesson lies its content; i.e., the information that needs to be transmitted or otherwise elicited. From this content should then emerge some understanding or concepts that will enable the students to confirm their knowledge by applying it to another arena of information, preferably some new instance with which they are unfamiliar. Then we will be satisfied that they have indeed learned what we set out to teach them. Lastly, in addition to specifying the desired knowledge and understanding involved, a lesson plan will stipulate the methodology by which this knowledge and understanding is to be obtained.

One can see how, once all this has been systematically explained, teaching is reduced to a mere adjunct, a turning of the crank to produce the necessary learning. Whatever genius may be required has been embezzled by the curriculum, thus rendering the teacher more or less superfluous. Why else would we need curriculum? Those who demand it, as well as those who sell it, offer different explanations. The purpose of curriculum, they say, is to ensure "continuity of instruction" among all students. Left to their own resources, teachers are evidently inclined towards individuality, which in education is considered dangerous, since not every teacher is similarly responsible or endowed. By combining forces we are able to exceed what any individual can produce. With a curriculum, moreover, we are able to enlist the kind of expertise that ordinary teachers simply cannot possess. Besides, once a curriculum has been installed, teachers are relieved from the heavy burden of creating daily instruction and are thus "freed" to pursue more creative activities.

The fallacy in such conceptions is the assumption that curriculum encompasses what students learn and that the role of the teacher is simply to transmit this learning as set forth in the curriculum. I would submit, however, that students do not learn curriculum because curriculum does not teach; we do. Curriculum is meant for us, not for them. The object of curriculum is to convey how teachers think about what they are teaching. This thinking constitutes the essence of their creativity, the center of their concern. It is the reason for having a curriculum because it is the kind of thing that only teachers talk about. Students worry about content, parents about achievement, administrators about policies, and school boards about money and politics. Teachers live and breathe curriculum because, when rightly conceived, it draws from them the entirety of their thought and the soul of their genius in capturing that thought and conveying it to others.

To teach, then, is also a work of genius and a feat of prodigious difficulty. To write about what we teach, setting it down so that others may know both the genius and the difficulty of our work, is an enterprise that in transforming instruction into curriculum permits teaching to outlive its teachers and so benefit all who would learn the agony and ecstasy of our humble calling.

Curricular Motives

I n our teaching journals we seek a level of instruction that does not have a name. Call this the level of **motives**. By motive I mean precisely what the dictionary defines as motive, namely, "*1. That within the individual, rather than without, which incites him to action; any idea, need, emotion, or organic state that prompts to an action. 2. A theme or dominant feature, as of a literary composition; a motif.*"

This seems to me a useful term in both senses of the given definition. To begin with, what we most want to know about teaching is what motivates it, prompts it into action. In the more traditional conception of curriculum such motives are incorporated inside the goals and objectives. Goals and objectives tell us where instruction is headed and what sort of behaviors it is designed to produce. But neither goals nor objectives tell us *why* they need to be reached or upon what perceptions they are based. They presume some prior state of being that needs to be changed, some idea about the way students think, some organic or developmental state that prompts them to act in certain ways when performing certain tasks. Underlying these presumptions are certain hidden perceptions on the part of individual teachers, perceptions that never get aired.

The value of journals is that they are designed to reveal individual perceptions about student behavior, perceptions that are induced from broad experience and that prompt us to teach in the way we do. They tell what we know about students and how we act upon that knowledge. This covers the first part of our definition that has to do with motivation— *our* motivation: the whys and wherefores of our teaching.

The second part of the definition takes on a different emphasis that generalizes upon the first. Here we address motifs—the dominant themes or features that underlie our teaching. In my journal entry on Art of the Essay, for example, I discovered *indirection* to be a dominant theme in my instruction. Were I to translate this motive or motif into a goal, I would have to say that I wanted students to become indirect in their writing, which although true is certainly not very helpful to anyone interested in the content or method of my teaching. For one thing, the goal neither reveals nor explains the perceptions upon which it is based. For another, it does not disclose the various layers of indirection that I am interested in pursuing, nor the relations that these layers may bear to one another. Lastly, a goal so stated does not make plain the singularity of its motivation as something I, and perhaps I alone, perceive, but instead parades as an unsubstantiated generalization.

In a recent conference with Beth Thompson and Jane Larsen regarding the Craft of Fiction, we found the notion of motifs produced some interesting results. One such motif related to the story in fiction. Students have to learn the difference between an event, an anecdote, and a story. They also have to ask, "Where's the story in this set of events?" They have to learn how to recognize when a story is "canned." I am not doing justice to these motifs here because these are not my perceptions and I have never taught this course. But were I to teach it, these are the kinds of things I would want to know. And after I knew them I would want to know what sorts of options I had for translating them into action. The idea of motifs comes closer to my notion of what curriculum should be than any of the traditional categories already familiar to us. That motives or motifs are first individual and second based on perceptions gained through classroom experience is what I find most appealing.

A world of difference divides goals, objectives, and "classroom activities," in traditional curricula from the idea of motifs, if only because the latter attempts to integrate the former in a personal way. Motifs try to articulate how we *think* about a course, not just how we deliver it. They tell how various elements are connected and orchestrated, how they are shaped and glued. This is the precious vein that we must mine in our teaching and our journals.

Essay Motif

In the spirit of exemplification, I here submit a journal entry for my course in Art of the Essay for the semester just taught. I am not suggesting that others be as long or detailed, but I found that once I got going there seemed to be a lot to say. This exercise helped me to place some of my teaching in perspective.

The Students

For the first time this year students in this course were comprised wholly of sophomores. The difference this made was immediately evident. It was, to begin with, a large class (25) housed in a small room (334), so that everybody was jammed together. Given the nomadic existence of student desks, there were times when a student or I had nothing to sit on. Besides the size of the class and the tightness of the environment, which enforced intimacy and conversation, perhaps a quarter of the students were clearly suffering from latent youth still under tenuous control. One could make a remark having no special relevance or profundity, and they would all turn to each other and start chatting and laughing. There were whistlers and drummers, free spirits and hustlers, all confirming the true meaning of sophomoric ("wise fool"). They were impervious to sarcasm and would cower into sudden silence only under concerted threat. I found this at once annoying and amusing, and would often observe them, trapped inside their own callowness. Yet there was not a scheming or sinister soul among them; they were simply ebullient to a fault.

Their intellectual qualities followed suit. They were active and intelligent, anxious to do well and to please, but lacking the calm and the subtlety that we so often find in our better students. They were fluent in speech, with flashes of insight or expressiveness irregularly sprinkled in their writing. They had obviously received much attention in writing and did not flinch when given assignments. They liked commenting on each other's papers and plainly were accustomed to that, but their criticisms were seldom enlightening or incisive. Their mastery of mechanics was tenuous. They did not know how to use semicolons, and their spelling—when unaided by computer—was unreliable. Although most of them were familiar with grammatical terms, they could not apply them with any confidence, with the consequence that fragments, run-ons, and comma faults were common. Among them, I would say that there were probably two or three who showed some advanced understanding of what writing entailed.

None of this did I find surprising, since I believe that mastery of the expository mode takes years to learn and perfect. But I saw that I would have to lower my sights a couple of clicks in order to remain on target.

The Program

As in past years of teaching this course, my aim is to emphasize the *art* of the essay, stretching the students beyond the merely acceptable and perfunctory kind of essays that had served them well enough in the past. Much of this art amounts to learning subtlety, indirection, and restraint, which, given the blatantly sophomoric character of this year's participants, made plain what work was cut out for me. These students are full of sweeping opinions, filled with bleeding emotion, but based on token evidence. For them, to persuade is to insist in a meager variety of ways. They are still puzzled by the difference between facts and opinions, thinking them vastly different. They will ask, for example, "Do you want the truth or just my opinion?" To which I would answer that I wanted only those opinions that were true.

Indirection begins in a couple of ways, the first being emphasis on details. The object here was to move them off the pedestal of their lofty opinions and get them buried in the details, the images, the events, and the objects that ultimately serve to contend more powerfully than mere opinion. They really have no idea how to go about this, much less *to* go about it. So they must first of all be convinced, which we do through readings and journals. I give them an "Author's Sketchbook"—one of those green, hardbacked notebooks—and have them describing stuff every day—some object, some place, some person, some incident, some conversation, some skill. I read and mark these, which is a real pain but the only way I can get them to take the assignments seriously. For them "description" is "boring," the kind of stuff they always skip over in the reading. They think description is dispatched through the use of adjectives, which I insist throughout amount only to "cheap details." I use McPhee and Agee and Updike and E.B. White to illustrate the use of details. We work on this *the whole first quarter*, which I think is the minimum one can devote to making a dent in their habit of blurring details with adjectives.

Indirection also manifests itself in sentence structure, which takes much longer to teach. All their sentences tend to go directly from A to B; they do not pause, do not elaborate, subordinate, qualify. To them, a nonrestrictive clause is a pure indulgence of adults who seem to have enough time to break the ineluctable rush from subject to verb to object. Nonrestriction is a waste of time, a garrulous appendage that complicates reading. So I pound away at "shelving" sentences, the piling up of illustrative absolutes at the ends and in the middle of sentences. Once again, I use the readings to exemplify—Hemingway, Stevenson, Montaigne, Chesterton, McPhee, and practically all writers. This in fact is the first lesson I teach. I ask them to make the longest sentence they can out of "She moves." They festoon them with breathless adjectives, all in a single pass. I tell them that this is the index one can use to tell a professional writer from an amateur—the ability to apply illustrative shelves. Naturally, this technique intersects with that of learning how to use details. When, for example, I show them the use of shelves by setting up the frame—"She moves, her _____, her _____, and her _____," they can complete it easily enough. But when I ask them what they thought of in contrast to when they first wrote the sentence, they readily reply that this second foray forced them *to visualize* the person they were describing, to which I add that its results also help the reader to do the same, whereas, before little such aid was provided in their initial efforts.

A third foray into indirection relates to narration, for just as they write their sentences, so do they tell their stories. They begin at the beginning and narrate to the ending. This reminded me of what our elementary school teachers call "Bed-to-Bed" essays, wherein children follow the rigid routine of the day from morning till night. Our students still have no sense of the technique for shifting the real time of the incident to improve its impact and its focus. One of the most successful papers I assign is to have them tell an incident from the middle, that is, to begin their story just short of its climax, then double back to fill in the necessary exposition, before returning to the climax to finish off the narration. For this particular assignment, I also insist that the meaning or significance or feeling about it be *implied rather than stated*. In other words, the meaning or significance must reside in the details.

A final element to the technique of indirection applies to their whole sense of what an idea is. For them, an idea is something already given and already received, hence more or less automatic. When a student insists that he or she "has no ideas," this is not merely a matter of lacking self-confidence; it is as much a matter of misunderstanding what ideas are and where they come from. So for the first quarter, I do not allow them to consider any "big ideas." I insist, and once again exemplify through readings, that ideas are not born but made, not taken from the head of Zeus but built one brick at a time. They must learn to write, I tell them, about things that do not already matter to people. On the contrary, their task as writers, at least in part, is to make seemingly unimportant ideas important. Here I delve into the first paragraph of Emerson's "Self Reliance," where he says (several times over in different ways), "Speak your latent conviction and it shall be the universal sense." These I translate into the phrase of the late psychologist Carl Rogers, who somewhere wisely observed that "what is most personal is also most general." We have a lot of fun with this assertion, since on its face it seems absurd. I could not find one student who would agree with me (Emerson or Rogers) about the truth of this assertion. How then, I ask, can there be any such thing as literature (a question they are not predisposed to ask much less answer)? It is, I affirm, a paradox, which itself requires explaining, for they cannot bear them, being themselves habitual proponents of polarity, masters of the excluded middle. This, of course, feeds into their problem with facts and opinions, which is why it needs to be discussed. All this I use as preparation for the persuasive essay they will not write until the latter half of the second quarter.

Grammar and Usage

I have argued elsewhere about the need to teach grammar, not just for writing but also as knowledge worth knowing in and of itself. For me, its application comes as part of the toolbox needed to undertake indirection. I have already said something about how they write from A to B in their sentences and the need to break them up. I have also observed their need to understand and apply both the mechanics of writing as well as subordination. In my estimation, they cannot apply these techniques satisfactorily until their understanding of sentence structure is founded on more solid ground. They cannot learn to use semicolons—which I call the queen of punctuation—until they can identify an independent clause. They cannot learn to punctuate an introductory adverbial clause or a conjunctive adverb if their understanding of sentences is based on their usage of them alone. Finally, they cannot have any grasp of *style* until they have a sense of usage, which is based on more or less arbitrary conventions rather than on grammar.

These are the kinds of things that they simply must learn. In all, I take about eight weeks to teach it to them—six for grammar and two for usage. I do not mean exclusive instruction but rather integrated instruction combined with their reading and writing. My students have written eight formal papers over the course of this semester, which seems to be about as many as I can stand correcting and amounts to approximately one every two weeks, lopping off a couple of weeks at the beginning and end. This combined with the Sketchbooks, mentioned above, individual drafts and sundry exercises, comprises what seems to me a goodly amount of writing.

I have used Maurine's curriculum for teaching the grammar, although I give a more elaborate treatment than I find there. It seems to me about right for these students, challenging but doable. I insist that everyone must pass the grammar, meaning that they take the test until they do. About a fifth did not pass the first test but they all passed the second. They did not complain about learning this, except initially. In fact, I think they enjoyed it. After we finished it, I would put a sentence on the board at the beginning of class, which in pairs they would try to diagram. They demanded these sentences beyond my interest in supplying them.

As for usage, I used the back of Sheridan Baker's *The Practical Stylist*, which has a review of usage very must like the one in our old achievement books. We simply went through the alphabet and at the beginning or end of class I would go over some of the more common instances. I gave them regular quizzes until we got all the way through. I am not convinced that they have learned all these wrinkles in the language, but what they do know is that there is a fund of particulars relating to language about which people hold strong convictions and from which they make uncomplimentary inferences about other people who don't.

Inside Reading

I use the ancient though venerable collection entitled *Essays Old and New,* by Jameson. I use this in part because up till now nobody else did and there were plenty of hardbound copies. I also use it out of nostalgia, since, incredibly, it is the very book I read in school when I was a sophomore. But mostly I use it because it has a fund of great essays, although many are now dated, as am I. There aren't enough essays by women—a total of two, I believe, so I have to supplement it, as I would have to supplement any other published text. By and large, though, it serves me well. We ended up reading nearly all the essays in it of which there are perhaps forty. I also asked them to select one of these essays for a paper on style, about which I shall have more to say later.

Outside Reading

I pause to note that two outside reading assignments were given, one consisting of essay collections listed for student choice and the other a reading front to back of a common issue of *The New Yorker.* For the first assignment students wrote a book review—not a "Book Report." For the second they took a test that surveyed their mastery of content and opinions set forth in that particular issue. The first is scarcely unique and is, I am quite sure, shared by those who teach the course, since we all pooled our bibliographies and published the compendium. The *New Yorker* assignment I did last year and chose to do again this year because I think it is valuable for them to know that people write essays for a living and that this magazine represents what I consider to be among the best in the world. I wanted them to have had the experience of reading it at least once. They struggled through it. I am aware that it is too sophisticated for them, but perhaps they will emerge from the experience knowing at least what we mean by sophistication. I did it to stretch them and stretch them it did, even though they found the jokes mildly compensating.

Style

It was from their reporting on the initial outside reading project, the one involving a collection of essays, that I got the idea about style. I had asked that as a part of their report they comment on the style of the author. I found their comments so airy and meager that it gave me cause to wonder about their understanding of the whole concept of style. After all, in every literature class the style of the author comes under some scrutiny. Although I was sure that they had heard about style many times before, it occurred to me that they were very far from grasping it. As with their general treatment of details, I found their commentary at the mercy of tepid generalities and trite adjectives. Style for them was either "boring" or "not boring." They gestured at style by uttering such profundities as "The author really gets his point across." Authors in question "did not use long words" or "hard-to-understand sentences." Their descriptions were "vivid" in that "they painted a picture in your mind." And so forth.

I found these so pathetic that I decided upon a frontal attack. They needed first a simple vocabulary that would permit them to talk about style, even if this amounted to saying that an essay was "tedious" rather than "boring." Despite knowing the meaning of words like majestic, lyrical, terse, plodding, contemplative, episodic, these were evidently not accessible to them. Nor could they break down the concept of style into its constituent parts, thus giving some range to the temper of their comments; e.g., tone, rhythm, organization, the use of figurative language, extended metaphor, satire, irony, assonance, dissonance, cacophony, allusion, active and passive voice, mood, diction. Clearly, one could not hope to teach all these concepts in a single semester, much less a year, but it seemed to me that their store of stylistic terms was so barren and wan that any effort to furnish such stores would be helpful. Neither did they have much idea about how to quote from text, much less *that* they should, as I had already made clear to them. They would carve out great chunks and treat them as if their stylistic attributes were so self-evident as to require no commentary. Yet they seemed able to pick out some of the more fertile passages.

We chipped away at passages that I would put before them, awaiting comment. We endured silences and squirming, desperate jabs. I would illustrate comments on style from readings. I had them look closely at Twain's famous remarks on "Fenimore Cooper's Literary Offenses," which they found funny but did not perceive the very careful and systematic work that supported them. Their papers showed some improvement, which was not entirely gratifying since nearly anything would have been an improvement. In another year I will try this again but with better preparation, more examples, clearer categories, more informal writing, and probably with some poetry, since many of these elements are most amply and elegantly illustrated there. For all this, however, we should not be discouraged nor overly surprised, given the nature of the beast characterized above. Style is itself a form of indirection and subtlety, both of which these students lack because of their bounding youth. It seems to me that sophomore year is not too early to make an organized assault if we expect them to consider style with much success in their senior papers.

A Room of One's Own

Early in September I had ordered *A Room of One's Own* in hopes of using it at some point in the course. That was before I had become fully cognizant of my students' competencies. I suspected that it would be too difficult, but thought it worth a try nevertheless. The opportunity to use it arose in the final weeks of the course. The class had written an argumentative paper and just finished a film review. Their final assignment, and final exam, would be a four-minute speech in which, not unlike most requests in college essays, they would try to reveal some focused aspect of themselves. Just as films would tap their natural obsession with the visual medium, the oral presentations would tap their natural inclination towards speech, emphasizing the importance of a visual audience.

That Woolf's *Room* was also a speech—actually a lecture—was only one of my reasons for inserting it at this point. I had obtained a taped version done recently on Masterpiece Theatre, which made it a performance that they could witness, just like their own presentations. But it is both the character and the content of the piece that were my main reasons for wanting to try it. To begin with, it is a brilliant piece of indirection, even taking in its more assertive segments. I wanted to demonstrate how essays might include narratives as this one does. Moreover, it seemed to me that as an essay it includes nearly everything that I had tried to teach. It is filled with stunning detail, as perhaps only a novelist could provide it. Her famous descriptions of Oxbridge, the meals she had there, her criticism of literature and its style, and, perhaps most important, her fabulous insights into the problems of the writer—all these I found bound up in this compelling little work. That it is generally seen as a feminist tract would surely add interest and partially compensate for the male dominance in *Essays Old and New.* Yet its greatest appeal is not as a feminist tract but as a humanist and indelibly personal tract, for it seems to me to contain more artistry and wisdom than any other single essay I know.

On the one hand this turned out to be a clever choice, given the commencement of the Gulf War and all the accompanying emotions and events surrounding it. I was able to show the tape during the height of the excitement. On the last day I read through perhaps a dozen passages I had marked, and in so doing indirectly summarized everything we had talked about throughout the semester. At the same time, however, it was partially wasted on them because they did not know enough to appreciate it. I did not have time to elicit their appreciation, so I simply told them what to appreciate. The piece clearly found its mark in some students and just as clearly went right over the heads of others. Still, I thought it went well enough to try again. I wanted to end strongly, as every essay should, and to leave them with something grand to chew upon.

Decent Exposure

This year as last I decided to diverge from the usual format for final exams in Art of the Essay. They had read forty-eight essays, commented on each of them in their journals, done outside reading, written eight formal papers, studied grammar and usage, learned three hundred vocabulary words, and tried to understand a dozen or so stylistic categories, all within a single semester. The exam would confront the most critical writing assignment of all—the college essay. Here they would essay to reveal some aspect of their character and beliefs to such as would ultimately presume to judge their worth as individuals and perhaps admit them into the circle of higher learning.

To aid them in ascertaining the impact of their essays, they would be asked to deliver them orally before their peers in the space of four minutes. To help them with the initial task of isolating some aspect of themselves that they might wish to talk about, I provided them with the following questions.

- Were you influenced by your childhood environment?
- Did some person have a great impact on your life?
- Have you been shaped by some unusual experience?
- Is there some activity that reflects the way you are?
- Can you be characterized by the work you do?
- Do you hold some special goal or purpose in life?
- Do you cling to some special value or principle in life?

All the tenets of good writing would be in force in their presentations: clarity of theme, the use of telling details, variation of sentence architecture, economy of style. Their essay would have to be written and submitted, but it would have to be delivered orally, not read.

However beastly the task, its purpose was beyond reproach, for sooner or later their composition skills would thus be tested and their futures in part decided by the quality of their responses. At issue was whether, amid hundreds of similar protestations that must be read, the uniqueness and depth of their souls could be discerned from such a piece of writing. This would put the art of the essay on trial, but I warned them about the plenitude of such stale topics as "My Trip to Israel," "Triumph at Camp Tochwah," "State Champions!" "My Brush with Death in the Parking Lot at the Mall," "Lost in the Himalayas," and the like. They would just have to peer into their hearts and search their meager pasts to see what they could find to talk about.

At the appointed hour, I placed myself at the back of the room, a lectern at the front, and called for the first volunteer. Nobody wishing to go first, they sat in tense silence, hoping some sacrificial lamb would take the first hit. I waited, then called out a name: "Elona Prilutsky, take the stand."

She flinched and turned horror-struck, as if having sustained a flesh wound. "Why me?" "Because you are the first," I said.

Realizing the futility of her resistance and the inevitability of her fate, she arose, walked to the lectern, and began to speak. When she was young, she said (unaware of the irony contained in these words), she had wanted to be like Carmen in Bizet's opera. Right now she looked as much like Carmen as I did—black leather jacket, bright red combat boots, wool tam-o-shanter, and underneath a wisp of green hair an angelic face. She admired Carmen because in the face of danger and intrigue she sang that "love is like a gypsy child that heeds no law on earth." It was that sort of freedom she had once longed for, but now she saw that in such freedom there was also terror. Although she did not further specify the source of that terror, we saw that she knew whereof she spoke and that the youth to which she had referred was a mask.

So began the hour, and as each subsequent speaker walked to the front to face the class without further prompting, we saw that this was indeed a convocation of unique lives now thrown together in a single room. One boy confessed that in pursuit of popularity he had mistaken competition as a way of gaining favor, only to discover that there was more to life than winning. Another said that what had begun as native talent had been squandered by lethargy, leaving him behind those who, although originally less gifted than he, had put their talents to better use. A girl chose as her hero her mother who after premature death of her husband had raised three children, educated herself, learned to ride a bike at fifty, and was taking yoga and piano lessons. A boy found in the recent death of his mother appreciation for all she had done— keeping house, paying the bills, caring for his invalid father—all of which had now fallen to him, and which, besides forcing his independence, had taught him the hard lesson of mortality. A few spoke of their reliance on friendship, how early on they had sought best friends only to have them forcibly removed, losing one to leukemia, another to adoption. One girl found in team sports the lesson that one cannot survive alone, that the world is too big and complex, the opposition too strong, to fend for oneself without love and support. Another valued above all the loyalty her family had taught her. Still another in learning to live with her grandmother had come to see the wisdom of an older generation. A Taiwanese boy sought mainly to help others as others had helped him. A few had gained through travel the perspective on how opulent yet parochial their lives had been.

We may say what we like about "kids today," but in my recent examination of them I am reminded once again that in spite of our best efforts it is always the children who save us, who bring our lessons to life and show us what they mean.

Calling Shots

W hen I learned to shoot a rifle in the service, having myself been forbidden from ever owning one, I was puzzled by the insistence of my mentors that every shot must be "called," meaning that after it had been fired you had to say where it went, even though the targets were too distant to determine this. The need to predict what could easily be determined later by inspecting the target seemed odd to me, even perverse. What I discovered was that one could learn to do this with surprising accuracy, once one concentrated on the moment of firing, which when done properly was always unexpected. One had to "holdem and squeezem" until the rifle went off, then to note where the sight lay at that exact moment. The theory was that if you did not know where the rifle was when it fired, you could not then adjust its fire the next time.

So, too, with writing. We have to know what we are doing as we are writing, but, more important, we have to be able to assess what we have done once our shot has been fired. Without this kind of assessment, we are at the mercy of those who finally view the target and tabulate how far we have drifted from the mark. We must learn to predict their reactions and compensate for them, a process we call "editing" (literally, "to give out") and revising (literally, "to see again").

Before I accept a paper, I ask my students to assess their work, point out both the strengths and the weaknesses that they see therein. These assessments are considered a part of the paper because, besides the actual writing, they include the student's vision of that writing, which I need to know when I advise them about what adjustments need to be made. It is the student's vision of that paper, rather than the paper itself, that I must address, for shorn of such a vision they are helpless. I see myself as teaching not "how to write" but what to look for and how to see, so that when I am no longer their captive reader they may see and write for themselves. Their manner of seeing determines my manner of reacting, eliminating the necessity of telling them things they already know and focusing on things they neither see nor know.

How many times have we been asked what we "want" in a paper, as if we had some preconception of precisely how every student should write every paper? "What do I have to do to get an 'A' on this paper" they ask, their presumption being that its supreme form resides already preconfigured in our minds, and that once revealed need only be copied without further thought. They want to be given the fish they should be learning to catch. It is the wrong question because it circumvents their need to learn what *they* want, as if their task amounted to writing our vision instead of theirs, thus avoiding the need to look into their own minds. What others may think of our writing is, of course, informative; it is always easier to judge and be judged by others than it is to judge oneself. But to my way of thinking teaching writing is no less a matter than teaching others to know themselves: to hold their sights, to squeeze their triggers, and to call their shots.

Fools of the Other Senses

I n his essay "On Knocking at the Gate in *Macbeth*," Thomas De Quincey says that "The mere understanding, however useful and indispensable, is the meanest faculty in the human mind and the most to be distrusted: and yet the great majority of people trust to nothing else; which may do for ordinary life, but not for philosophic purposes." He cites as an example a request to draw two walls standing perpendicular to each other, or the appearance of houses lining either side of a street. Without instruction in rendering perspective, we allow our understanding to overrule our eyes and are unable to produce a satisfactory representation of what we look at every day of our lives. After all, perspective in drawing had to be invented.

Whereas De Quincey's quarry is understanding *Macbeth* by attending to his longstanding intuition about its effects, mine is a similar understanding of why students must be taught to describe what they see. Given the charge to describe and their choice of what to describe, they will invariably produce persons who have no faces, buildings that have no architecture, trees, furniture, plants, plots of ground, conveyances—all in an unrelieved generic mode. People are tall or short, their dress formal or casual, their bodies fat or thin, their manner shy or cool, their hair long or short, their age old or young. Nature generally goes by color alone—grass is green, sky is blue, night black, flowers red, sunsets pink—all of which is dutifully judged to be beautiful in a generic sort of way.

Were we to infer from these manifestations the cast and configuration of the world in which our students live, it would approximate something out of *1984*, a world devoid of distinguishing characteristics, uniform in texture, homogenous in shape and tone, featureless.

Surely it is not their vision that is at fault, nor yet their attention, for when it comes to judging the precise tint to be desired in jeans, the dazzling hue of fingernail polish, the trick swirl of hair, the minute differences in accoutrements for hi-fis or cars, they are staunchly purist in their tastes. It is their attention that has been diverted. That to which we habitually attend is analogous to standing at the foot of a gravel path that stretches out to the horizon. Whereas pebbles at our feet are individual and distinct, our ability to distinguish them diminishes inversely with the distance of our gaze.

Mindful of De Quincy grappling with his understanding, however, perhaps it is more accurate to say of students that they have reached an age where they tend to see not what they look at but what they understand, that in a sense their writing is altogether too *rational* in its presentation of the world. We know of young children their inexhaustible interest and astonishing acuity in what they see. I recall my toddler daughter once remarking that the exhaust of the car in front of us cast a shadow on the ground below. Similarly, a walk with one of this age is a slow walk indeed, filled with interruptions and minute examination of objects all but invisible to us. But with adolescence comes the emergence of generalization and the consequent blurring and merging of distinctions once so near and dear. Shorn of their curiosity and grasp of the particular, our students are slaves of the generic, reveling instead in categorization, dichotomy, stereotype, and summary opinions.

In teaching students to write, it does no good simply to admonish them about being specific, for in gaining the power of generalization they have lost their capacity to see and celebrate specificity. This is what makes their understanding "the meanest faculty in the human mind," hence, "the most to be distrusted." We can do no less than teach them to see again, to "revise" their vision. They must rediscover the evidence that their eyes faithfully deliver but now shunt directly to their understanding. To them the world has become suddenly transparent, for they have been taught to see through its surface detail in order to contemplate its meaning, having learnt our lessons all too well. Now they must learn to catch themselves seeing again, to look at what they see instead of seeing what they look at. As Macbeth himself says, "Mine eyes are made the fools o' the other senses, or else worth all the rest."

First Books

E verybody, I suppose, can recall that book in whose pages was first revealed the chasm of things that lay in wait beneath the print as the eye stumbled unassisted across the page. There were other stories, of course, lovingly read aloud by devoted souls, and early on one watched in detached wonder as grown-ups waxed motionless and silent under the spell of the voice that spoke to them inside their heads as their eyes danced over print. Otherwise animated and responsive, before these pages they became strangely transfixed and removed as if they were somewhere else.

I must confess that in my early days, when some children I knew had already taken to the classics, I developed a violent distaste for reading. Part of it may be ascribed to my fascination with what was already at hand, a world much too interesting to forgo on the odd chance of becoming engrossed in another that didn't actually exist. Why read a book when one could climb a tree, ride a bicycle, roller skate, play cops and robbers or kick the can? There were local battles to be fought, mischief to be made, concrete skills to be mastered. Besides, reading for me was arduous and slow, requiring one to sit still. Comic books I could tolerate because I could understand them with minimal reference to the print spilling out in the spoken bubbles. But my mother, herself a reader, thought comics injurious not only to the eyes, but also to the moral fabric, foreboding premature and catastrophic decay, thus forcing me to hide what comics I could acquire or forage elsewhere among the rich collections of my similarly debauched friends.

Besides, none of my heroes was a reader. You never saw Tom Mix curled up with a book, and the Lone Ranger only read notes handed to him by Tonto. My father read only the newspaper and Time Magazine, which was forgivable because both were relatively brief and because he said he needed to know what was happening elsewhere while he was at work. Besides my mother, the only readers my age were either girls or the few guys who couldn't play baseball, usually either the smart ones or the oddballs. I looked upon them with pity as congenital misfits, never suspecting their reading to be the cause of their academic success. These would be the ones who would later describe themselves as "voracious," which always sounded to me like a debilitating condition, leaving its victims no other way to learn or to live save inside a book.

I read only when I was sick, which in those days was a fairly regular and predictable occurrence, communicable diseases marking milestones in one's normal maturation—chicken pox, measles, mumps, whooping cough, croup, tonsillitis, flu, and the rest. Then, with shades pulled, windows cracked against "night air," milktoast and tea, and supper brought up, one would resort to reading just to break the crushing monotony. It was then, too, that my mother, desperate and clever as she was, would bring me books, crisp new ones with pristine jackets on them, still redolent of fresh print.

Trapped as I was, a prisoner to my disease, weakened, usually swollen and lonesome, it was then that I read my first book: *Silver Chief: Dog of the North*. On its cover against the deep blue of the arctic night stood a silver dog on a moonlit silver landscape. Inside on the first page was his portrait, smiling with soft brown eyes and small silver ears, looking as if you were just about to stroke his handsome silver head. I had never seen a silver dog. I checked for other pictures to see how far I would have to read and how much I could understand without reading. It looked interesting and negotiable, so I began and read straight through, stopping only to eat.

Until recently, what it was about this book that so enthralled me I could not precisely recall. I wish I could recount how, having the world of books suddenly opened, I thereafter became a voracious reader. That the book made a deep and lasting impression cannot be doubted, but upon regaining my health I fell into my prior ways and did not become a reader until well past adolescence when reading became as much a necessity as an inclination.

Truth is, I did not think about the book or revisit it until about forty years later as a teacher when I was finishing up a senior English course. As a final exercise in the waning weeks of May, I asked my students to talk about the book that had influenced them the most. It was a gratifying assignment that they undertook enthusiastically, yielding an intriguing array of works: Shakespeare, Dante and Dostoyevsky, Austen and Bronte. When we had finished, one student asked what book had most influenced me. Without thinking, I said, "You mean besides *Silver Chief: Dog of the North?*" The name simply came to me full-blown out of nowhere, and thereafter became a kind of standing joke among us. Recently, a very good friend with whom I had shared this story took it upon herself to obtain me a copy, a first edition published in 1933.

One evening, on holiday and browsing my shelves in search of another work, I happened upon it. Too early to retire and too late to initiate a larger undertaking, I sat down to leaf through it, looking at the pictures once again and trying to recall the story. For the second time I read it straight through, this time in a single sitting. Then it all came pouring back: Sergeant Jim Thorne of the Northwest Mounted Police, garrisoned at Fort McDonald, is given his orders from Inspector McLoed to track down the varmint "breed" named Laval, wanted for robbery and murder. He sets out for a lone cabin in the arctic wilderness where he meets and gradually tames the wild and canny Silver Chief—half husky, half wolf—who ultimately saves his life, helping him to find, subdue, and finally bring to justice the cruel and shiftless Laval. By their own affirmation, "The Mounties always get their man." As things turned out, with a lot of help from a silvered quadruped, they also got me.

"The mental qualities we most admire in all human beings except our several selves," said Charles Sanders Peirce, "are the maiden's delicacy, the mother's devotion, manly courage, and other inheritances that have come to us from the biped who did not yet speak; while the characters that are most contemptible take their origin in reasoning. It is the instincts, the sentiments, that make the substance of the soul. Cognition is only its surface, its locus of contact with what is external to it."

Things You Find Nothing About in Books

These past few months I had occasion to imitate one of my favorite literary characters and learned a thing or two. The character is Thomas Macwhirr, Captain of the good ship Nan-Shan in the story "Typhoon," whom Conrad describes as "having just enough imagination to carry him through each successive day, and no more . . . ," an observation that might apply as well to Mozart or Picasso as to Macwhirr, depending on the day. "Yet the uninteresting lives of men so entirely given to the actuality of bare existence,"Conrad reassures us, "have their mysterious side."

It was not that Macwhirr was unfamiliar with books, for when confronted in the China Sea with clammy heat, a beastly swell, and a plummeting barometer, he rightly concludes that "there is some dirty weather knocking about," and consults a volume on storm strategy. Characteristically, his book says, the center of great storms bears eight points off the wind, but since there isn't any wind, this advice is rendered useless. "It's only to let you see," he says to his first mate Jukes, "that you don't find everything in books."

As junior captain of the good ship Yonder, as new and fit as the Nan-shan, I found this observation apt. Much of my prior courage at sea, I discovered, derived principally from sailing other people's boats for short periods of time. Piloting one's own craft in strange waters is another matter. I saw, too, that in comparison to other craft one finds in these waters, ours was decidedly meager, hardly worth the massive fittings festooning their spacious decks. However meager or grand, I was also reminded that "all these rules for dodging breezes and circumventing the winds of heaven" come to naught when faced with nature's fury. There is no emergency cord to pull, no place to stop and get off when the going gets rough.

The morning of hurricane Bob we were in Onset, located at the west end of the Cape Cod Canal, having been denied a mooring the night before and advised to seek shelter elsewhere. Not knowing where the center of the oncoming storm would hit, we could not decide which way to go. At three thirty that morning we were wakened by the sound of engines, and coming up on deck saw a parade of large motor craft heading out. My instinct was to find some place to hide, some narrow inlet or creek one could ply and tie the boat to a big rock or thick oak on the shore. Consulting Eldridge, the yachtsman's bible, we were told only to get off the boat, since boats, as the book laconically observes, "are replaceable."

We left just before dawn, the weather just as Conrad had described it— red dawn, the air so clammy with moisture that the sides of the boat were running with condensation, absolute calm. The full length of Buzzards Bay lay between us and homeport where our mooring lay, comprising twenty miles of waters notorious for their gales and choppy seas. Following the path of the canal, whose massive lighted buoys looked like a giant runway, a gentle breeze came up, barely rippling the surface of the bay, which for the first time I saw devoid of a single craft. Had it been blowing, we would have been kept busy, but the eerie calm was unnerving. "A gale is a gale," says Macwhirr; "there's just so much dirty weather knocking about the world, and the proper thing is to go through it with none of what old Captain Wilson of the *Melita* calls 'storm strategy.'" We warped on sail, opting to make the best of the fair wind to speed our meager craft on its lonely way. The wind steadily increased, forcing us first to reef and then to douse all but a portion of the jib. The boat, driven by wind and engine, flew. It would have been exhilarating had we not known what lay behind, pressing north and destined to slam into the coast.

By the time we reached port the squalls had begun, gradually obliterating both sea and land. We were glad to get off the boat, hastily making what preparations we could imagine to get us through this particular day and its heralded hundred mile an hour winds. I could not find in books how to secure a boat, one of perhaps three hundred in the harbor, against such an onslaught. "Don't be put out by anything," says Macwhirr to young Jukes, "Keep her facing it. They may say what they like, but the heaviest seas run with the wind. Facing it—always facing it—that's the way to get through."

Like the Nan-shan, our boat did get through, facing it, still afloat with a couple of holes punched in the hull and her rails bent and twisted by other boats torn from their moorings and bearing down on her. After the storm, ninety-six boats had been blown ashore, looking like so many beached whales. In recounting the adventures of the Nan-shan in a letter to a friend, Jukes writes, "The skipper remarked to me the other day, 'There are things you find nothing about in books.' I think that he got out of it very well for such a stupid man." We did, too, much the wiser. Onset, we later learned, was inundated.

In teaching we are pilots of our own crafts, plying uncharted waters. Among the things we find nothing about in books is how to teach, how to cope with all the dirty weather knocking about. Much of the advice we hear stipulates ways for dodging breezes and circumventing the winds of heaven. Macwhirr had just enough imagination to foresee that "the heaviest seas run with the wind," not against it, and consequently that our course is best laid by facing what lies in store. When speaking of art, Cynthia Ozick appears to echo these sentiments. "Knowledge is not made out of knowledge," she says. "Knowing swims up from invention and imagination—from ardor . . . Sensibility (or intellect, or susceptibility) is most provoked when most deprived of scaffolding; then it has to knot the sheets for the climb."

Although there are many things we find nothing about in books, fortunately, there remain a couple of things that we do.

Autumn River Run

With the compass needle resting on southwest, I look over my shoulder once again to check my course, heading for Bramble Point, a name I have given to a bump of land marking a bend in the Concord River. Oars at the ready and seat at three quarters slide, I prepare for my return run, two miles back to the landing. Full autumn now, only the oaks retain their stiff and tawny leaves, the maples' bare branches etched in silver against the background of evergreens. Were this not my neighborhood, I could swear I was in Saskatchewan.

A flick of the wrists drops the blades into the water as I uncoil to overcome inertia in two shortened strokes. With the third stroke I lengthen to full reach, my hands swinging outboard of the gunwales, pressing my chest hard against my thighs. At the catch where the feathered blades are squared and dropped I concentrate on the pull-through, ensuring that arms, legs, and back work in unison to finish the stroke together before hands drop down and away, sweeping the oars back on their return to complete the cycle. The handles of the oars thrown quickly forward pull first the shoulders and then the tail out of the bow, causing the boat to run out from under me, much as any small craft will leap forward if, standing on the bow, one runs towards the stern. As I slow my momentum approaching the catch, I hear the familiar rush of water beneath me and see the wake behind as the parted currents rejoin like hands clapped together, pushing up a little white rooster tail.

Checking the compass that sits in front of my feet, I adjust the course a couple of degrees by pulling a little harder on the right oar. The trouble with rowing is that it must be done backwards, with the consequence that one cannot see forwards. Having a compass eliminates the need to crane the head around, which breaks the rhythm and tips the boat. This in turn may cause one to "catch a crab" by allowing an oar to plunge so deep that it gets caught in the water rushing by and cannot be extracted. In an eight-oared shell, where both the speed and the momentum are amplified and the leverage of the long oars reversed, catching a crab can lift a man right out of his seat and throw him over the side.

Passing "The Rock" that sits just offshore like a large turtle, I prepare for the upcoming turn occasioned by Bramble Point where I must alter course some thirty degrees to keep in the middle of the river. This section of the Concord has been designated a federal wild life preserve, its banks still wild and unsettled. It is the very section that Henry Thoreau so admired in *A Week on the Concord and Merrimac River.* To the right out of the corner of my eye I see the Georgian mansion once occupied by my landlady with its preserved elms and manicured lawns. Next comes the house I had rented from her, now obscured by the swamp brush that has been allowed to grow unattended. From here I had gazed upon the river and its traffic for thirteen years, yearning for a craft like the one I now occupy that would enable me to ply its waters.

I suppose at one time or other every boy around these parts thinks about building a boat but is impeded by the complexity or the impracticality of such an undertaking. There is something terribly elemental, something primal about making one's own boat. For years this had been my secret desire, the Concord River running as it did so close to my house. I wanted a boat I could row; not a skull exactly, but something I could propel at an advanced rate, something approximating the feeling of all those years I had spent in school rowing on crews, a craft that would emulate the lightness and beauty of those sleek wooden shells that slid so swiftly and silently upon the waters.

Such a vessel, however, being so fragile and unstable, could never be a family craft. Oarsmen are perforce loners for whom rowing is a kind of mystical experience in which one feels the craft a part of one's body, the oars an extension of one's arms, and the rhythmic motion a kind of mantra demanding total concentration. Children would rock the boat, spouses would want to talk, guests to stop and look at things. To purchase, much less construct, such a craft would therefore be a selfish act, unsociable and never fully understood because it could not be shared. Then, too, there was a certain danger in venturing out alone on water in such a delicate vessel, leaving the family behind to worry and wait for one's safe return. So I relented, deferring and repressing my boyhood dream.

But as the years amass and the children disembark into their own lives, priorities shift. Because age itself impels us ineluctably towards increasing jeopardy, we come to view danger in a different light, losing our fear of extremity or untimely demise. Similarly, others learn to tolerate in the old what they are also willing to excuse in the young.

Sensing my advantage, I bought a kit for my last birthday to celebrate my advancing years. It came in a long thin box in which I found lengths of plywood, pieces of mahogany frame, screws and fiberglass, epoxy glue, a length of nylon rope, and a small coil of wire. It looked like an oversized model airplane kit. That from this rather ordinary collection my future craft should emerge seemed to me remarkably improbable. Nevertheless, I immediately set to work, dutifully following directions, anxious to see my belated prize take shape.

First you glue up the sides, making from two lengths a sixteen-foot span approximately one foot wide. Then you attach the triangular stem pieces, which, when held together at each end and sprung out in the middle, create the desired shape of a narrow, double-ended skiff. Once three or four frames are glued in at regular intervals and shaped blocks attached on the bottom of the bow and stern, you have something that for all the world begins to look like a real boat. With the boat laid upside down on its gunwales, you now bend on the flat pieces of precut plywood that will become the actual bottom. The bottom and the sides are now stitched together at the chines with short lengths of wire that are passed through holes you drill at the edges of the bottom and the sides. Pulled down tight, the stitching rounds the bottom as it approaches both the bow and stern. Finally, you glue and glass over this stitching, then cut the wires on the inside and remove them. It is a fairly primitive yet ingenious process.

As this work proceeded, the skiff rapidly took on a life of its own. I was astonished each time I descended the cellar stairs to find this boat waiting for me, as if it had somehow been there all along and had magically sprung into existence. To discover a long sleek craft waiting down in the cellar was not an experience I could quite take in, so anomalous was it among the lawnmower, the table saw, and the porch furniture. It seemed as if someone had mistakenly misplaced this prized possession, it having somehow gained entry on its own, as if from Kansas.

I decided that the insides of my open boat should gleam with the warmth of varnished wood to give it a yachty look. Outside it would be sapphire blue, a hue I had always admired in other people's boats. But fairing the lines of the hull turned out to be more of a job than I had anticipated, ensuring that there were no sags or lumps in its surface. Oddly enough, it turned out just as I had imagined.

The stalks of swamp grass on my left tell me that I am approaching the final bend, marked by the Brothers' Rocks on which are engraved the names of Dudley and Winthrop who were granted these lands by Charles I. Cutting the bank close, I swing to one hundred and eighty degrees for the final run, my arms and legs tightening from exertion, my layered clothes now soaked through, slightly chilling me from the cross wind. The trick now is to maintain form in the face of mounting fatigue, pressing the mind to control the rebelling body. Keeping the Brothers' Rocks on the point of my stern, I try to relax on each stroke's return, letting the boat run out before I propel it forward once again. Two men in a boat unexpectedly loom up on my left, an aluminum craft with a barge bow and equipped with a huge outboard and raised plastic seats that look like barstools. They do not look up. Strange how much money men will spend in order to catch small unsavory fish.

The sound of cars on the bridge signals my approaching destination. I lean into the oars and take up the stroke. Hyperventilated, the air now smells sweet as I taste salt from the sweat running down my cheeks. My sturdy craft alternately lifts and drops with the rhythm of my motion. As the landing slides into view, I cease rowing and with the oars aloft let the boat sail.

Thus traversed, the river is mine once again. The wonder is that I had waited so long to gain such a simple pleasure from this elemental vessel, knowing now that dreams should not be too long deferred lest once attained we do not leave enough time to savor them.

CURRICULUM

Alpha and the Beta

Something there is about curriculum that teaching evidently abhors. It is almost as if teaching could not abide captivity, as if once captured, instruction were programmed to expire. To be sure, not all curricula are equally discerning nor elegant in design, though each has been fashioned to fill some need, and most have at some time been taught with zeal. Yet in every school we find shelves and files stuffed with materials moldering in disuse. That the course of education should be swung by political and economic concerns is probably inevitable. That it should on occasion defer to fashion is, though less defensible, altogether human. But that curriculum should suffer such speedy attrition as our laded shelves and files attest is plainly unconscionable.

While it is clear that no single increment added to the bulk of material swelling our schools stands much chance of improving education, it is a mistake to account curriculum as among the excesses of a prior age and to dismiss it on these grounds as something already tried. What we have discovered, or perhaps only rediscovered, is that curriculum is far easier to write than it is to teach. Nor should we accede to the notion that by holding teachers suddenly accountable for what they teach we shall meet with certain triumph, where before we encountered only apathy and caprice. Accountability means that learning counts only when it can be counted. By succumbing to addition, however, the quality of teaching—to say nothing of teachers—is not automatically enhanced.

The crux of the matter lies in the way we define curriculum. Here etymology of the word offers some clues. Literally translated from the Latin *currere*, meaning "to run," curriculum means "a running." This reminds us that the value of curriculum lies in the running, not in that which is run; in runners rather than in racecourses. Thus, we can think of curriculum chiefly as something to be shared, something that in seeking a common goal also demands individual pursuit. But it is more a relay than an individual race we run, for the life of curriculum depends on the personal link that binds its participants in overlapping pursuit—the writers with the teachers and the teachers with the students. In relaying content one to another, they work momentarily in tandem, the new recipients gaining the momentum that their partners relinquish.

Shorn of metaphor, curriculum essentially amounts to a series of exchanges, which, though focused in the classroom, also precedes and follows what happens there. It is a continuous process of transferring experience in increasing detail to ever-widening audiences. Both the advance and the attrition of curriculum depend upon their success in negotiating this exchange. Given enough freedom and encouragement, most teachers can teach a course of their own making successfully. It is when curriculum changes hands that it most often breaks down, for unless teachers can externalize their strategies, filtering out the alchemy of their personal experience, their style and zeal, their teaching will turn to ashes in another teacher's hands.

By the same token, teachers do not need to be told how to teach and look with disfavor upon curriculum that obviates or inhibits their need to create. More than anything, teachers want to know what to expect from their students, how to cope with potential questions and responses. Only those who are willing to relinquish their invaluable experience can provide this kind of information. If teaching harbors abhorrence for curriculum, it is because curriculum writers invariably treat their experience as if there were no other, and are thus inclined to prescribe a solitary course of action.

To speak of curriculum, then, is to speak of creativity and exchange. But how does this exchange come about, and to what end does creativity aim? To begin with, there is that part of curriculum that is already in place in every school, the curriculum that commands our attention every day. This is the stuff we teach, irrespective of the discipline under which it falls or the manner in which it is gathered. Call this side of curriculum "Alpha." Alpha curriculum reminds us that we must make certain conscious decisions about what we do in class every day. Whenever we make up a test, get up an assignment, lead a discussion, choose a book, or design an activity, we are engaging in alpha curriculum. When an English teacher decides to read *Othello* instead of *Hamlet*, a biology teacher decides to postpone dissection, a math teacher to alter the sequence by taking up trigonometry before logarithms, or a shop teacher to defer individual projects until students have learned to use the lathe—all such decisions fall under the alpha of curriculum.

In contrast, "Beta" curriculum signals a new departure from the mainstream of disciplinary policy. Generally tentative and exploratory, beta curriculum tends to be innovative, even revolutionary. This does not mean that imagination or creativity is the exclusive province of the beta; the difference lies in the way that imagination and creativity are applied. Beta tends to be more intensive in its demands, since it seeks to establish some relatively undeveloped domain within the discipline. Most often, beta takes the form of a new course or program. In science, for instance, a new offering in oceanography may be launched, or in English a new elective in minority literature. Perhaps foreign language and social studies agree to undertake a program in Asian studies, or occupational education opts to develop a series of courses in computer programming. Such efforts would fall under what we have termed beta because they require extensive planning and special support, probably some research, as well as some sort of higher administrative approval and community review.

So defined, this division of curriculum into alpha and beta need not be sharp nor especially precise in order to prove useful. Its purpose is to provide a way of looking at curriculum as a whole and what we do with it. Because what we have called alpha comprises the bulk of curriculum, for instance, we could argue that it should receive the bulk of our attention. Yet such is not often the case. It is rather the beta that captures our attention because in breaking away from the alpha it offers us the chance to start anew and overcome the limitations that the alpha now reveals. Despite the weight of evidence to the contrary, we hold out the hope that the beta will somehow escape the pitfalls that dog our current efforts. The alpha constitutes what we already know about the status quo, whereas the beta holds all the promise and excitement of the unknown. That the beta is also likely to derive support from its currency in the press or professional literature also works to its advantage. Moreover, teachers are likely to find the beta more alluring because it offers them the chance to distinguish themselves, to enjoy greater independence, and to develop special expertise.

For all these reasons the beta absorbs the better part of our efforts to improve instruction. Instead of trying to perfect what we already have, we are inclined to abandon the alpha and pursue the beta. The unfortunate result is that curriculum is kept in a constant state of suspension and flux.

Yet the beta is not without limitations of its own. In departing from the alpha the beta involves a heavy commitment of time to develop new strategies and materials, time that would otherwise be devoted to perfecting the alpha. Moreover, in severing itself from the alpha the beta incurs the danger of becoming isolated. Beta curriculum tends to become identified with its originators who sometimes end up being saddled with their own success. If their course becomes popular, other teachers must be enlisted to cover additional sections, teachers who have had no part in creating the curriculum and are therefore indisposed to teach it in place of something else. Lacking either the experience or the zeal of the creators, the adopted teachers will be hard pressed to match the curriculum's prior success. If they fail, then the chances of the beta surviving are seriously impaired, and it is likely to disappear as soon as its originators either lose interest or move on. If they succeed and the course becomes established, then the bloom of innovation is bound to fade, and the course effectively becomes an alpha with all its attendant problems.

Clearly enough, neither the alpha nor the beta can flourish alone. It is their relationship that becomes crucial, and this relationship must be characterized by exchange. Creativity without exchange is ultimately self-defeating. Alpha without beta is like soup without seasoning, thin and bland. Beta without alpha provides more sauce than meat. The alpha and the beta are therefore interdependent, each in its way serving to keep instruction alive. Alpha is evolutionary; beta, revolutionary.

Our mistake in the past was to think that the alpha could somehow be replaced by the beta, that they were mutually exclusive alternatives. And so in launching the beta we dismembered the alpha, only to discover that the beta was no better, merely different. Having concluded the beta a failure, we exhumed the alpha, resuscitated it, and scotched any further attempts at beta.

The wiser strategy appears to fall somewhere in between. We need to recognize the alpha as fundamental to instruction. However implicit and seemingly routine, the alpha constitutes our only vehicle for perfecting instruction. What's more, the alpha serves as a watershed for the beta. As part of our commitment to continuing excellence, however, we also require the beta to help us test out new subject matter and techniques for teaching. Although innovation is by no means the exclusive province of the beta, teachers nonetheless need the freedom to experiment and the incentive to take risks. As long as the alpha is being actively sustained, we stand to gain from the brand of innovation that only the beta can provide.

Just as our assessment of the alpha is determined by how amply it feeds the beta, so must the beta be gauged by how well it is assimilated into the alpha. Once linked in tandem, like runners in a relay race, the alpha and the beta may thus together reach the omega that has ever been our object.

Standards of Instruction

A difference divides curriculum from instruction that is too often overlooked. Sarah's mother seeks a conference with her English teacher about the amount of homework assigned because answers to her queries seem always to be either that none was assigned or that it has already been done. Or perhaps William's father seeks a conference to complain about too much homework being assigned, William staying up all night to finish his assignments. A syllabus will specify the content of a course—the novels to be read, the periods of history to be covered, the units of science to be taught. A curriculum will additionally specify the skills to be acquired, the concepts to be mastered, the methods of presentation, the manner of assessment to be administered. Conversely, there are matters of instruction that fall outside both the syllabus and the curriculum, matters that need to be addressed by departments and conveyed to parents and students alike.

Call them Standards of Instruction. Such standards comprise the assumptions collectively held by teachers of a particular subject or discipline regarding the ways in which instruction is to be conducted across individual years or sections. These assumptions should be collectively held but also commonly derived and/or reviewed each year by all teachers involved. We distinguish *instruction* from *curriculum* by stipulating that the former refers to the delivery of the latter, namely the ways in which a subject or discipline is commonly taught. This does not mean that individual styles of teaching are either abrogated or discouraged, nor consequently that everyone is expected to teach uniformly. It means that members of departments, and in some respects the school as a whole, share certain assumptions regarding the particulars of instruction.

In the teaching of English, for example, there needs to be agreement among the teachers involved about the quantity of reading assigned over a given period, about the number of papers assigned within that period, about what teacher comments on papers generally include, about the teaching of vocabulary and grammar, poetry and usage, essays and drama, about the mix of methodologies enlisted, the use of conferencing, of technology, the employment of notes, the recording of assignments, and so forth. Individual teachers may wish to teach different books, assign differ kinds of papers, but the quality and number of books read, the quantity of writing assignments, the treatment of mechanics will be similar if not the same.

In this sense Standards of Instruction are similar to class expectations that individual teachers maintain except that they are collectively held across all classes within a discipline and are intended to serve several purposes. To begin with, they are intended to maintain the quality of instruction in school, making clear to teachers, students, parents, and supervisors those expectations that are shared regarding the teaching of all subjects. Notice that by standards we do not mean aims or objectives, which have to do the mastery of skills and content in a given subject area and are therefore curricular rather than instructional.

A second purpose of these standards is to ensure the optimal degree of continuity among classes. Although the actual content of a freshman course may differ in various respects from class to class in regard to the books read or the topics of the papers assigned, by and large a student's experience in one class should duplicate that of students in other classes in regard to the amount of work assigned.

A third purpose would comprise a general agreement among teachers and supervisors regarding the grounds upon which evaluation should rest, thus eliminating any surprises or disparities about general expectations. We don't want teachers criticized, for instance, for not reading enough books or assigning enough papers. Once the standards of instruction have been delineated, supervisors should adhere to them in their evaluations. If they regard these standards as insufficient, then they need to convey this to the department as a whole. At the same time, when a teacher's assignments fall behind those of others in the department, there can be no argument about whether that teacher is justified in failing to meet the standards set forth.

Similarly, once Standards of Instruction have been articulated by all departments, supervisors can determine how these balance collectively across all disciplines so that students do not suffer from the disparities.

Publish or Emperish

On a day very much like her seventeen previous first days of school, teacher Fran Wacht walks into Room 341, carrying a cardboard box full of books. Rested and tanned from her summer vacation, she slides the box onto the top of her desk, slings her purse on the back of the chair, smiles warmly to the crowd of young faces focused upon her, and greets them with a mature and silken voice: "Good morning!" The students shift in their seats, mumbling a staggered response. Wheeling energetically to face the board, she grasps a full stick of chalk lying in the tray and writes in a graceful, cursive hand.

Autobiography
Ms. Wacht

Still smiling, she turns and says, "My name is Ms. Wacht, and this is Autobiography, D Block." Removing her bright red gradebook from the contents of the box, she retrieves the banded green and white computer list, unfolds it, and says, "Now let's find out who you are." Tall and slender, her jet black hair falling straight past her shoulders in front and back, she is poised and neatly dressed, with a sparkle in her dark and deep set eyes that conveys both warmth and assurance. As she reads the names, the students identify themselves by flagging the palms of their hands and quietly saying, "Here," whereupon Ms. Wacht looks up, examines their faces intensely for a moment, then smiles and nods while entering a check beside the name.

However familiar the ritual, there is something unique about this class that distinguishes it from all other classes Fran Wacht has taught in her seasoned career. That uniqueness waits inside the cardboard box now sitting on her desk. Completing the preliminaries, she distributes the books, each one a crisp and shiny 8 1/2 by 11 paperback, sepia with dark brown lettering. Down at the lower right hand corner an oval wedding portrait displays a couple in a rather stiff and formal pose: he with top hat, white tie, and long double-breasted coat; she with modest white veil, high collar and three-quarter sleeve white dress, clutching a small white evening purse in her left hand. Wearing tight but firm smiles, the couple at first appears to be shaking hands, or just finishing, but at second glance they are modestly holding each other's hand. It is a picture of Fran Wacht's grandparents. The title reads,

I REMEMBER:
An Autobiography Text
For High School Students

Pleased to have new copies for once, the students quickly leaf through the text, stopping to look only where there are pictures, all of people: Margaret Mead, Eudora Welty, Nicholas Gage, Elie Wiesel, Maxine Hong Kingston, Mary McCarthy, Helen Keller, Lillian Hellman, Senator Paul Tsongas, Anne Frank. What they do not notice is that names of other authors whom they take to be unknown are actually names of fellow students and a couple of faculty members. Nor do they notice right away that the name on the front cover is identical with that of their teacher. Finally, one outspoken girl pipes up: "Ms. Wacht, did a relative of yours write this book?"

"No," says Ms. Wacht calmly, "I wrote it." As she watches her words sink in, she knows that she is suddenly in a different place than she has ever been, and that those three little words were worth every minute she had spent in the last two years compiling her work. Even though she had taught the course on and off for ten years and knew it well, she had never known it this fully, for in having to write everything down that she wanted said she discovered that she had far more to say than she thought she would at the outset. And now, at last, she had finished. Before her on every desk lay her reward: a visible manifestation of her work for all to see and to study. Everything she wanted was there, complete, ready to be taught: the readings, the assignments, the projects, the bibliography, the explanations, the concepts. For once in her life there would be no waiting for the Xerox, no collating and stapling and filing and distributing, no lost or extra copies, no harried typing and running off copies. And the look of surprise, even incredulity, on her students' faces confirmed that with those three little words—"I wrote it"—she would be able to take this class the distance that she herself had traveled, word by word, and now knew so thoroughly.

And that wasn't all. Articles in local papers would appear with her picture—"Brookline Teacher Writes," "Teacher Publishes Her Own Textbook," "BHS Teacher Pens Her Own Textbook," "BHS Teacher Writes Classroom Text." At Steve's gas station she would become the local celebrity—"Let's not keep THE AUTHOR waiting!" Her family and friends would want autographed copies. She would speak at professional conferences about teaching autobiography and about publishing one's own text. She would get up a mailing brochure about the book to answer inquiries and would receive correspondence and orders every day. Meanwhile, in the halls or cafeteria she would overhear students comparing English teachers, and one would say, "Oh yeah? Well my teacher wrote a book just for *us!*"

In these days of homogenized materials and "dumbed down" texts, having one's teacher write her own book for a class is certainly refreshing, if not unique. For years now textbook publishing has been dominated by the giant multi-nationals who, by catering to the whims of selection committees, seek to capture the markets in Texas and California. With the development of "readability" formulas, difficult words have been removed, such as "inalienable" from the Declaration of Independence, and schoolbooks that exceed the ninth-grade reading level have become a rarity. Similarly, anything that smacks of controversy—or worse, ambiguity—has been expunged from pages that are set before America's youth. *The Wizard of Oz* has been accused of promoting witchcraft; *The Diary of Anne Frank* of suggesting that all religions are equally valid. Biology texts shy away from mentioning evolution, fearing it will offend those who advocate "creationism." In trying to appease every special interest group, and so escape controversy themselves, commercial publishers have transformed beyond recognition the world that students are ostensibly being prepared to enter.

For students in Fran Wacht's class, however, the world that awaits them is real because it is a world she has lovingly prepared for them, the one that both she and they know and can discuss. They will learn to write because some of the works they will read have been written by students from their own school and their own town. They will see how such common experiences end up not only in books, but also in the writings of well-known authors. They will want to write because they know that their own teacher has written, and because they know that in her writing they will hear her voice and imagine her talking. For them, writing will be at once most personal and most general. And, who knows, if they write well enough, maybe one day other students will read and admire what they have written.

But besides the obvious benefit for the students, there are unanticipated rewards for the teacher as well. Writing persists as one of our most effective instruments for learning, which is undoubtedly why higher degrees in education retain theses and dissertations as validating exhibitions of competence. Written composition draws knowledge from us, transforming the tacit into the explicit so that we come to know what we think by seeing what we say. To publish is to make public what we would otherwise be satisfied to keep private and unexamined. In forcing us to express our ideas, writing enables us to test them and discover their impact. While there is always the hope that our readers may find recompense in what we say, it is we ourselves who derive the greatest benefit from laying down our words on paper. Writers must write for themselves before they can reach others.

In writing her book, Fran Wacht has come to see the worth of what she knows and what she does. Recognition of teachers is so often extraneous to teaching itself, since instruction is fleeting and largely unwitnessed except by those who are in most need of learning. Consequently, teachers gain notice largely for what they do outside of class—organizing car washes, sponsoring picnics, advising clubs, coaching sports, directing plays, chaperoning dances, serving on committees—all of which make public their activities. Unless it is somehow published, however, classroom instruction automatically perishes as a series of isolated events that must be recreated every year for a private audience.

In effect, by publishing *I Remember*, Ms. Wacht has written the autobiography of her own course. "After years of feeling that everything about your job is intangible," she says, "at last they know what it is you *do* for a living." Having teachers shed their instructional anonymity is not among the concerns currently at issue in schools. Reformers worry instead about requirements that teachers need to fulfill before they can be certified to teach. Or they propose elaborate schemes for testing and evaluating teachers to determine if they have reached prescribed levels of excellence. Yet curiously, what teachers do when they are not meeting requirements, taking tests, or being evaluated is not considered especially relevant, since decisions about content and method fall outside their purview. The substance of instruction is left for commercial publishers, selection committees, elected officials, administrators, or appointed commissions to decide.

A profession presupposes something to profess, some specialized body of knowledge or application of skills that calls for exercise of judgment and discretion. More than a command of arcane facts, or homilies about interpersonal relations, teaching demands intimate understanding of how knowledge is best conveyed. In denying its practitioners responsibility for exercising this understanding and relying instead on outside authorities, schools effectively reduce teaching to little more than a trade. Whatever prestige may be attributed to titles or credentials or even to salaries, the status of a profession ultimately resides in its power to determine and express the nature of its own expertise.

If teaching is emperished for want of publishing, teacher publication is also more accessible that it has ever been. Where manuscripts once had to be laboriously typed and retyped before reaching final form, the advent of the microcomputer has rendered this process far more efficient. Word processing delivers into the hands of the writer the flexibility to store and endlessly revise text with accuracy and speed. In effect, the prior distance separating the writer from the printed page has been radically reduced, so that it is now possible for text to be shunted directly from monitor to printing press. This development has diminished not only the time involved in publishing, but also the cost, since the intervening step of typesetting, which was among the most time-consuming and costly components, has been virtually omitted.

Besides technology, an embryonic industry known as "individualized publishing" and "print on demand" brings publication a step closer to reality. One need no longer convince a mammoth publisher that the envisioned text will capture a significant portion of the sprawling national market. Without editorial restrictions or massive sales forces, these companies will print as few as 150 copies of texts, be they anthologies, study guides, or curriculum of any sort comprising labs, tests, readings, assignments, bibliographies, maps, pictures, or whatnot. Print on demand services store manuscripts on servers and print individual copies as required. Content can be either copyrighted or original material or both. If material is copyrighted, the publishers will obtain the requisite permissions and include any fees in the overall cost of the book, which depends on the number of pages, copies, and fees. Since the school comprises the market, authors/editors pay nothing for the publication of their work; the price of the book is the cost of publishing it. Nor need they wait for a year before they see the fruits of their work, for once materials are submitted it takes only a few months to deliver the finished product. This compressed turnaround time allows for revisions on an ongoing basis with each subsequent printing.

Here, then, is a way to circumvent the corporate giants and obtain a text designed especially for one's students, a text that contains nothing extraneous, but at the same time includes whatever may be deemed appropriate. Because the publishing process has been greatly condensed, one need not postpone publication until some appointed time in eternity when everything will be known about a course. The text can develop in stages, altering content with each printing to match student responses. And should the text warrant broader exposure, then the latest volume can be submitted to a larger publisher as concrete evidence of the author's achievement or design.

But what about the quality of these materials? Can teacher published texts match those that are commercially available? If Fran Wacht's autobiography text is any indication, the answer must be "yes." Of course, there will not be as many pictures nor perhaps as much research, but neither need there be concerns about "readability" or blandness for fear of offending scattered pockets of persuasion. If members of the community object to a teacher published text, they won't have to lobby the school board or go to court; they can call up the teacher/author and discuss their reservations. At least they will be able to discover what is being taught and why, whereas, with the use of commercial texts they have no way of knowing how closely the teacher is following the text, if at all.

More important, purchase of teacher published texts is an investment in teaching. It goes without saying that teachers who take the trouble to write their own texts will be better teachers than before, not only because they are bound to learn a great deal, but also because of the impact their efforts will exert on colleagues as well as students. If these efforts prove disappointing, then the school can work to improve them, which is more than can be done with commercial texts. Better still, by investing in their teachers rather than in commercial publishers, schools grant those teachers the kind of professional recognition that cannot be drawn from daily instruction.

In the process of writing her book, observes Ms. Wacht, "I experienced many of the same feelings my students experience when they sit in front of a blank sheet of paper with a new assignment in the offing. I'm sure I made as many false starts, crumpled as many pieces of paper, became frustrated, and worried as much about deadlines as many of my students do. I grew more aware than I have ever been that if you truly want to find out what you think or feel about something, you should write it."

We have heard enough about elevating the profession. The time has come to take our careers into our own hands and profess in print what we teach in class so that students and teachers alike may everywhere derive the benefit of our experience and hard work.

After the Dittoes Fade

S tuart Dunbar remembers the old days when part of a teacher's duties included filling inkwells in every desk from a copper watering can. Now retired, he also remembers not only when students were required to use ink, but also when teachers were obliged to *make* it. First you dumped the blue-black powder into a pail, then filled the pail with water and stirred until all the lumps smoothed out. Inserting a funnel into a gallon jug, you filled it almost to the top, taking special care not to spill it, and *voila*, ink!

Similarly, when the process of spirit duplicating was introduced, teachers had to make their own "dittoes" one by one. Back then they were called "hektographs," *hecto* being Greek for "hundred." Stuart swears he was never able to squeeze anything like a hundred copies from a hektograph (more like twenty), but it went something like this. Once the copy had been manually typed on a master, you shifted it to a pan shaped something like a cookie sheet that held a slab of gelatinous substance treated with glycerin. First you sponged the gelatin damp and then laid the master on it, carbon side down and waited for a couple of minutes. Removing the master, you took the first copy sheet and placed it on the slab, applying even pressure with a roller especially designed for that purpose. You then peeled back the paper, starting with one corner, and presto, one copy! Being slightly damp, the copies tended to curl into cylinders, and when several masters had been impressed on the gelatin, you had to heat the pan on a hotplate to erase prior impressions.

Ah, for the good old days when everybody learned their lessons in quaint Norman Rockwell edifices, savoring the selections from McGuffey's Fifth Eclectic Readers: the prim and bespectacled matron at her desk, class arrayed in rows before her, seats screwed to the floor, the pupil at the blackboard, the map on the wall, the flag in the corner, the pencil sharpener on the windowsill. While we no longer make ink or turn out hektographic copies by hand, even in this burgeoning computer age teaching remains an essentially paper and pencil operation.

Consider what is involved. In the normal course of teaching, regardless of the texts that may or may not be available, "handouts" must be created; e.g., assignments, tests, quizzes, readings, bibliographies, exercises. Easily one third of a teacher's time is devoted strictly to clerical tasks—typing, duplicating, collating, stapling, distributing, collecting, filing, retrieving, and recording. Once the content of their handouts is written—itself a time-consuming task—the text must be duplicated, then distributed in class, extra copies being preserved for absentees, lost or discarded copies. The amount of paper consumed in the course of a year at an average school will fill a typical classroom from floor to ceiling. And this does not include the paper generated by the students themselves in assignments.

Dittoes next came with a carbon backing sheet already attached. Once cranked by hand, the "modern" ditto machines, many of which are still extant in schools, are electrically driven. Even then, the number of legible copies one could eke out could not surpass the hektographic limit and still be read. Imagine the limitations this imposed on the resulting curriculum. One could not share a ditto with one's colleagues without relinquishing the future copies it might produce. Conversely, attempts to save the master ended with the carbon gradually seeping into the paper so that duplicating additional copies the following year yielded print resembling forty-year-old tattoos.

Moreover, the process by which these copies were hastily prepared on clunky manual typewriters invariably produced a harvest of errors, each of which invoked the following satanic chore. First, you remove the sheet from the typewriter and locate the error (written backwards) on the back of the sheet. Then you take a single-edged razor blade—coming thus equipped—and carefully scrape off the offending letters, taking care not to smudge them in the process. Next, you rip off an unused corner of the carbon backing sheet and try to insert it directly under the error just removed. Reinserting the sheet carefully in the typewriter so that the loose corner does not slip down, you locate the exact place on the page where the original error still appears on the front and retype the word or letter in question. Because our standard Remington, Royal, or Olivetti typewriters—between whose keys one's fingers could easily slip, creating another error—had no half space, adding an additional letter to a word that originally appeared without it required consummate skill.

Is it any wonder that so many handouts placed in the hands of children were error-ridden and/or illegible or that so many typewriters in the school were tinted purple? And, of course, every teacher eventually experienced the disaster of forgetting to remove the tissue separating the facing sheet from its carbon backing, making the whole exercise utterly wasted and requiring the handout to be completely retyped.

The only saving grace was the vapor that freshly minted dittoes exuded, granting sniffing students a momentary high as they passed the copies back through the rows. But the astounding implication of this duplicating process was that it had to be virtually repeated *every single year.* Curriculum, in other words, had to be annually and laboriously reproduced. Purely as a matter of efficiency and survival with this ludicrously inefficient process, curriculum was seldom if ever shared.

Enter the Xerox. Few will deny the enormous impact of this machine on teaching, even though it initially entered schools as a tool of administration. Suddenly, it was no longer necessary to type every handout on ditto or stencils (remember *stencils*?). Multiple copies of articles, excerpts from books, or original handouts could be run off on this miracle machine. The hitch was that teachers were initially considered interlopers, since the machines were originally purchased to serve administrative functions. Further, because there was usually only one machine to a school, the waiting lines grew longer and the machines began to break down more frequently from overuse, for which the teachers were blamed. In comparison to the ditto, the Xerox simplified and expanded the range of materials reproduced for class; e.g., pictures, graphics, different styles and sizes of print. And today, these machines further ease the clerical burden of the teacher by automatically collating and stapling documents.

Enter now the computer, once again through the threshold of administration, this time in the service of attendance, report cards, scheduling, memos, and the like. Here data could not only be copied but also created and endlessly manipulated. Initially prohibitive in cost and recondite in operation, computers spawned their own breed of specialists, a priestly class who spoke an arcane language (Fortran, Cobol) and performed their wizardry in eerie grottoes filled with humming, blinking slabs of electronic paraphernalia. Unlike the ditto and the Xerox, access to the world of computation demanded knowledge of its operating systems. As such, it was a natural for schools, for besides being a machine employed to perform administrative tasks, it was also a subject that could be taught and a vocation that could be acquired.

For teachers, however, creation of computer science became a major impediment to computer use. It meant that computers were a specialty in which one had to be trained like any other discipline. Despite introduction of the microcomputer, the personal computer, and the home computer in which much of the arcane content of programming had been bypassed and the prices slashed, the aura of "high tech" persisted, frightening away all but the most inquisitive. And when schools began to speak precipitously of computer "literacy" and to declare computation a "basic skill," teachers became further convinced that Apples were not for the teacher but for the nerds in the new generation that would be born with silicon chips in their mouths. The majority of teachers remained "happy primitives," for once the redoubtable Apple IIe's rolled into the classrooms, their worse fears were confirmed, the students taking to them like ducks to water while in crash courses in computer literacy their teachers sank like stones.

A product of his times, Stuart Dunbar ended up very much ahead of them. By the time he retired he was teaching Fortran on the school's mainframe computer. While we no longer make ink or turn out hektographic copies by hand, teaching remains essentially a primitive operation. The computer, the fax, the scanner, our email, and the Internet notwithstanding, we still type on the same Qwerty keyboards used by Mark Twain. Ironically, with our present capacity to produce errorless text, the ditto has come back into its own as the quickest, most accessible and least expensive means of duplication.

We must remind ourselves that, for the most part, schools remain fairly antediluvian organizations. The revolution in technology has ostensibly removed any excuses for not surpassing prior epochs of educational achievement. Today we have at our fingertips the power to bury our progenitors in paper. Never mind "multimedia," Powerpoint, DVD, and the rest. Equipment that works in schools must be rugged, accessible, simple to operate, and inexpensive. Like knowledge itself, technology is most effectively applied when it is invisibly woven into the fabric of our thoughts and everyday routines. The amount of information that computers can store and instantly deliver is potentially unlimited. The trouble is that computers cannot tell us how to use the vast array of information they offer. No matter how big the screen or how rich the audio, the computer cannot conduct a discussion, cannot comfort, defer, cajole, wonder, or decide. In other words, it cannot interact emotionally or intellectually. Education demands the kind of live interaction that no computer can replicate. What works in the living room or the boardroom does not wash in the classroom. Students learn because they want to be like those who teach them, whoever those people may be—parents, teachers, friends, artists, or artisans—and whatever the means by which their instruction is delivered.

The Second Revolution[4]

L ike its proverbial antecedent, the road to technology in education has been paved with good intentions. As is customary with most technological innovations—the steam engine, the phonograph, the telephone, the motor car, the radio, the rocket—computers began as intriguing oddities, ingenious toys that provided specialized entertainment for the idle and challenge for the inquisitive until a practical use could be found, some menial task they could perform to relieve us from our more primitive endeavors. In their formative stages of development these inventions have always proved more trouble than they were worth, often intensifying our labors, yet seductive enough in theory to warrant expanded use.

My own introduction to computers occurred in the late sixties in a graduate course on computational linguistics. Although my interest lay more in the linguistics than in computation, I was set to work on programming a massive machine that hummed in an otherwise darkened and hushed facility where a youthful and rather condescending instructor held sway. The assignments I remember well. We were asked to write one program that would translate English into Pig Latin and another that would look up a word in the dictionary. I found these assignments mystifying and frustrating in the extreme. For one thing, they aimed at performing a task that I could already do with far more speed and facility than trying to replicate my mental processes in a machine. For another, I found it difficult, if not impossible, to "think" like the machine, which would invariably produce erratic and unpredictable results, unforgiving of the slightest error or oversight.

Barely passing, I emerged from the course disenchanted and perplexed, both by my own failure to master this new medium and by the meager potential it seemed to offer. An early lesson one learns from computers is how literal and obtuse they truly are. They can do only what they are told and every step must be so tiny as to eliminate any possibility of misconstruing one's intent. They know nothing except their own arcane instructions and are consequently incapable of assuming anything about the real world. In this preliminary state of mind, I found it difficult to imagine any useful purpose to which my newfound experience might be put. Teaching with a computer made about as much sense to me as recruiting kindergartners for building a space station.

Imagine my dismay, then, in hearing my superintendent announce a decade later that computer skills would henceforth be considered "a basic skill" that every child would be expected to master. By this time the microcomputer had arrived, and, ever mindful of fashion and modernity, my school system had floated a bond to purchase one hundred and fifty Apples for our elementary schools. These children, we were solemnly informed, would be delivered to the high school "computer literate," and we would be expected to harvest and prune these important skills. Having to teach children something they already knew more about than we did was not an altogether enticing prospect.

Our concern was premature, however, for initiation into these mysteries did not go smoothly in the elementary schools, the teachers there having been given only the most cursory introduction to the secrets of Logo, which they had been assigned to teach after a few hours of orientation. Their sessions had been punctuated with crashes and conducted by those barely more expert than the teachers themselves. Subsequent sessions designed to orient the high school staff did not come off any better, and indeed, convinced our teachers that the Wonderful World of Technology was sufficiently alien to ensure their never touching a computer again. Fortunately, our business department had moved energetically to annex this new field, teaching courses in FORTRAN and ordering two $10,000 Wang "word processors" to train prospective office workers. For the time being computation would safely remain a specialty for those who sought employment opportunities in the field, leaving the rest of us to conduct business as usual.

In the ensuing years, however, computer technology continued to explode. IBM launched the "Personal Computer," Lotus the spreadsheet, Ashton-Tate the database, Word Perfect and Wordstar their processors, and Apple the redoubtable IIe. Still scarred from my early experience, I chose to compromise by purchasing a dedicated word processor that resembled a large production typewriter with a brain—16K of memory, beautiful print, and, after a fashion, many of the word processing features that were becoming standard. Instead of a screen, this machine had a small, rectangular window across which trudged a single line of luminous type. In addition, a separate disk drive, using 2 1/2 inch disks, provided potentially inexhaustible memory.

It was on this machine that I began to realize the real potential of computers. For the first time in my career I did not have to retype my whole curriculum every year in order to update handouts for class. Like so many others, I had once been wedded to the ritual of the well-sharpened pencil and the yellow pad, scratching out text before committing it to type and then revising and retyping it to produce "the original" on my venerable Olivetti, long encrusted with droppings of whiteout. On my new machine the copy came out sharp and clean, headings embolded, titles underlined, bereft of embarrassing typos. With time, instead of having the machine type out each line after I had written it, I learned to type out the whole piece just by watching the type parade across the little window, thus gradually weaning myself from the habit of seeing my text immediately on paper. My writing gained in fluency and speed because I didn't have to worry about the typing and could concentrate on my thoughts, knowing that the errors could be rectified later.

Today, with continued development of the technology and steady erosion in prices, what was once arcane and frightening has become increasingly transparent. Although the only simple computer constitutes the one we happen to know, we speak now of megabytes and megahertz as we once did of 78, 45, and 33 rpm records. Similarly, software, shareware, and groupware are growing as familiar as the old Decca, Capitol, and Victor record labels. Now we can routinely order hardware and software by email rather than from the local computer vendors who had so recently played such a critical role as our technological advisors. Our fingers have gradually lost the strength required to pound out a piece on the old Royals and Underwoods, and the programs that once took days to install and months to learn now seem quite intuitive to us as the user interface gropes towards standardization.

Although this technology has begun to seep into our veins, it has yet to penetrate our hearts. There remains a lingering suspicion of machines, a latent fear of operations that we can no longer see or feel, and still some foreboding about so much power that can be manipulated with so much facility. With this burgeoning power delivered to our fingertips comes the counterpoising dread of losing control over a world that has become too fluid and complex to understand or retrieve. Our hearts echo the cries from Walden to "Simplify, simplify," despite the spreading networks and telecommunications that daily lure us further abroad from our books and prints. With the current introduction of "Multimedia" we wallow in a virtual world where, in the words of Macbeth, "function is smother'd in surmise, and nothing is but what is not."

As with any change of this magnitude, we have also begun to question the ends towards which these changes tend. Although the relative costs of basic computing have plummeted, they have been offset by the increasing sophistication of the equipment we buy. By any measure computers are expensive, not only to buy and install, but also to maintain and replace. Whereas initially we were satisfied with 64 kilobytes of memory, cheap television monitors, printers that would type in both directions, and the ingenuity of saving text on cassette tapes, memory and speed requirements have increased exponentially, making 64 megabytes a paltry sum. Today we demand hard disks, crisp color monitors, and laser printing. Add to this the mounting costs of funding multimedia presentations, networks, telecommunications, and CD-ROM, and we can safely project that the use of technology in education, at least as the industry would have us conceive it, is rapidly drawing out of reach, especially in times of recession and fiscal austerity.

Besides matters of cost, the proper role for technology in education and its impact on learning are still at issue. In the early days of the revolution I recall an advertisement on television depicting a disheveled young man disembarking from a train, a man who had evidently committed the egregious error of attending college without benefit of a computer. In the ad we see him returning defeated and crestfallen to rejoin his disappointed family and face a clearly diminished future. Such ads were calculated to strike fear into the hearts of parents who foolishly deprived their offspring access to the wonders of technology. The ad, incidentally, was for the Adam computer, a $500 wonder whose tenure on the market was as troubled and brief as that of the college student portrayed.

As the blush of promise has begun to fade from technology, now is the time for us to take stock and decide for ourselves what is next. Clearly enough, the first revolution is over: computing has become both personal and pervasive. But like most revolutions, this one will take as much time to sort out as it did to occur. That technology will continue to grow and expand need not be questioned. As the behemoths of yesteryear grow smaller, cheaper, and ever more powerful, they will become appliances found in every home. As children of today become the teachers of tomorrow, technology will become ever more internalized and intuitive among its burgeoning users. And as applications and refinements continue to emerge, we shall find technology spreading into every corner of our busy lives. The first revolution may be over, but the second revolution has just begun.

What might this second revolution have in store for schools? It has often been said of computers that they are a set of solutions in search of a problem. I have seen schools fully equipped with labs used solely for teaching typing—banks of computers functioning as almond Underwoods. Conversely, when labs are properly used, they are invariably overbooked, affording too little access for individual students to master their skills. What is becoming clear is that personal computing need not dictate that schools supply every person with a computer. Neither need they invest the huge sums required to obtain the latest gadgetry. As the root of the word itself tells us, technology means "the theory, principles, or study of an art or process." A second revolution in technology calls for schools to proclaim ownership of their own internal processes and determine for themselves what problems technology can help them solve.

Take communication. How many times has it been said in faculty meetings that students and staff alike must learn to communicate? How many problems have been blamed on "lack of communication" between students, staff, parents, and the community? And how many times has everybody vowed to communicate better? Communication, after all, lies at the very heart of learning. So why does it keep coming up where learning allegedly presides?

The answer in part is that schools aren't designed for communicating. Quite the contrary. In different places at different times and for different things, everybody is neatly tucked away behind closed doors. Teachers meet with their classes each day, where only one person at a time is allowed to talk, then send their students home to grapple with problems. Once home, neither students nor teachers are accessible to each other, often when they most need to be. If they want to communicate, they have to set up another meeting, which means finding a time when no one else is meeting, like after school. Because after school is the only time to meet, however, no one can find the time to meet then either. The joke is that whatever happens in schools is determined by the bus schedule. The irony is that although teachers talk all day long, they have no time to communicate, either among themselves or with individual students.

Take another problem. What is all this talking in school actually about? The answer is that nobody really knows because there isn't any way to know. There is a curriculum, to be sure, replete with goals and objectives, and there may be daily lesson plans as well, but what is actually being taught, to say nothing of learned, can be observed in only one place at one time. The rest is hearsay and perforce inferred. But if we cannot know exactly what is being taught in schools at any given time, how can we expect to assess, much less improve, the education our students are receiving?

Perhaps the greatest service technology can render to education lies in these two areas: communication and curriculum, both of which go hand in hand. Much like books themselves, computers are essentially buffers, meaning that by encoding communication they earn the capacity to defer messages between the time they are sent and the time received. The important difference between books and computers is that, whereas the former are static and unchanging, the latter are fluid and evanescent. Thus, a book can be written at one time and place and read in another, carrying communication through the ages and across our continents. Once written, however, a book's content remains fixed. Not so with computers that have the capacity to defer the very process of writing between the keyboard and the printer so that there is no longer any such thing as "the original." Once digitized into the binary code, computer input is fluid, taking the shape of whatever medium we choose, be it visual, acoustic, or even tactile. Transmitted through electrical charges rather than chalk or ink, computer input gains not only in speed and versatility, but also in its capacity to be minutely stored for instant recall.

It is these features that render such technology a boon to education, for they enable us to transcend the limitations of time and space that imprison every school. Computers give us time to communicate because they need never sleep. They remember what we tell them, translate and transfer our messages at any time of day or night. They thus have the capacity to link individuals across time and space without forcing them to meet. Schools equipped with a network of telecommunications become schools without walls where learning can continue after the bell and in spite of the buses. Teachers equipped with computers at home and at school can create and preserve and revise and convey their instruction in forms hitherto denied them. They gain access to resources both within and outside the school. Curriculum thus becomes constant and fluid rather than static and periodic, enriched by the work of others, enhanced in its form and presentation, manageable in its progress and assessment.

Our mistake in applying technology in the past has been threefold. To begin with, we viewed computers as the objects rather than the instruments of learning, thinking that literacy entailed learning to program their internal codes. As the face of technology became more transparent and "user friendly," we saw how it could be employed in helping us do what we were already doing, easing the teachers' clerical burden of developing and producing instruction.

Our second mistake has been to wedge technology between the teacher and the student, making machines the medium instead of the instrument of instruction. Bypassing teachers is the same mistake made with nearly all technological innovations applied to schools—the radio and television being our most recent examples where teaching was confused with talk and naked information was misconstrued as knowledge. To the contrary, whatever the medium, learning must be fundamentally personal, genuinely interactive, and indelibly humane.

Our final mistake with regard to technology has been to allow administration to take precedence over instruction. Where attendance is recorded, moneys expended, parents notified, and policies made, there are we likely to find the latest technology in use. Teachers and teaching come second, usually making do with leftovers and hand-me-downs. Had administrators to perform their own clerical tasks as teachers do, technology in schools might have kept pace. Teachers might have been given their own computers as part of their professional equipment. They might have received the kind of education and training demanded of every work force bent on elevating its standards of performance. Computers confined to the main office do not serve the main purpose.

Schools today have enough technology at hand to begin the second revolution. It is a revolution not so much in equipment as in thought, not in new things to do but in new and better ways of doing the things they have always done. As the instrument of thought, technology is the linkage of minds in the enterprise of learning.

The Pinioned Swan

Ever since Leibniz, who is alleged to have been the last man to know everything, interdisciplinary study has suffered a steady decline. At a time when formal learning was far less common and cumulative knowledge much refined, one could cross disciplinary lines with impunity and plumb the depths of inquiry in a variety of fields. Today, the idea of interdisciplinary study has managed to gain in appeal what it has already lost in applicability. Like the pinioned swan, it is a beautiful thing to contemplate, but has been rendered too cumbersome to fly.

The lure of interdisciplinary study lies in its potential for integrating our disparate inquiries, each of which pursues its chosen quarry in relative isolation. So fragmented and specialized has our present enterprise become that it enables us to major in something only minor, thus gradually loosening our grip upon the whole. In effect, because we choose to learn more about less, education gradually plucks our wings until we lose our capacity to soar.

Why not, then, set out to learn less about more? Why not confront knowledge as a whole and see where it leads us? Reasons abound. To begin with, the organization of our schools does not permit us to pursue learning in this way. Departments are held accountable for the portions of knowledge assigned to them. They cannot broaden their outlook without shortening their syllabi, thus risking fulfillment of their appointed tasks. And besides, whenever the question of cooperation among departments arises, it raises the problem of who is to pay for the added instruction and how such instruction can be scheduled. The solution often takes the form of courses taught back-to-back, such as American literature and American history. Alternatively, a single course in humanities will endeavor to encompass several subject areas, such as art, architecture, music, dance, history, and literature. While both these solutions constitute an advance, they scarcely suffice to carry the potential of interdisciplinary study to fruition. They are, in fact, multidisciplinary rather than interdisciplinary.

A more profound limitation to our pursuit of the interdisciplinary is that it is the kind of inquiry we do not know how to conduct. Since every teacher must be trained in a specialty, none is equipped to inquire into the whole. This is why our attempts at interdisciplinary study are in fact multidisciplinary, for what we bring with us is a disciplinary view of the whole rather than a view that cuts across disciplines. Our predicament therefore amounts to this: *we have no exemplars of the education that we collectively espouse.* Although every teacher presumably exemplifies the level of knowledge that may be attained in his or her respective discipline, how many teachers exemplify the ideal of the educated person as a whole? Can we honestly demand a level of mastery of all subject matter from our students when we ourselves cannot reach, much less exceed, that level? Either the notion of the educated person is a myth, or we are its pretenders.

In the face of these limitations, what reasons have we for not dismissing the notion of interdisciplinary study altogether? Primarily three. On the most practical level we need to find a meaningful way for teachers to talk to each other, and thus to relieve the chronic sense of isolation within a discipline. The cries for "greater communication" among faculties everywhere in schools is a need no one can deny, but also a need that never seems fulfilled. What is required is not simply talk but something significant to talk about, something central that we all share in common and that we feel an urge to know. Neither behavioral objectives nor classroom management, that something is clearly education as a whole, our own education as well as that of our students. Teachers are nothing if not learners; it is the only thing they really care about.

This brings us to our second motive for promoting interdisciplinary study. Because we are all teachers who are unevenly learned, what we have to offer each other is our expertise, both individual and collective. Enough is known in every faculty to fill a decade's worth of in-service agendas. If we would each exemplify the education of which we are a part, then it is high time that we got cracking. How many English teachers know the thrust and impact that quantum mechanics now exerts on our modern conception of reality? How many math or science teachers are comfortable with poetry or are familiar with the insights that great literature offers to all ages? How many languages does every teacher speak and how much history do they know? It is unbecoming, indeed, contradictory for an educational institution to view learning at any level as complete.

Our final motive for interdisciplinary inquiry is perhaps the most compelling. "Break the pattern which connects the items of learning," said Gregory Bateson, "and you necessarily destroy all quality." And in his preface to *The Ascent of Man,* Jacob Brownowski confirmed as his ambition "to create a philosophy for the twentieth century which shall be all of one piece." Inasmuch as it fails to connect the items of learning, our pattern of education is broken, our philosophy in pieces.

What is at stake is *wisdom* plain and simple, wisdom in the sense that Alfred North Whitehead once defined it, namely, as "the way in which knowledge is held." Wisdom is the pattern that connects individual items of learning. It is the ambition that transforms the pieces of knowledge into a philosophy all of one piece. It is, as Einstein succinctly phrased it, what we know after we have forgotten everything we have learned.

Education is the receptacle rather than the content of learning, the way in which knowledge ends up being held. The aim of education must therefore be its shape rather than its substance. And that shape must perforce be interdisciplinary. If departments cannot serve as appropriate vehicles for interdisciplinary instruction, then we must seek out alternative structures and find a way to schedule and support them. If we do not know how to conduct real interdisciplinary inquiry, then we must seek out alternative structures and find a way to schedule and support them. If we do not know how to conduct real interdisciplinary inquiry, then we must take time to learn. The educated person cannot be convincingly displayed in parts; each of us must instead represent the whole of which we are but a part. Without primary feathers education cannot fly

Patterns That Connect[5]

"**B**reak the pattern which connects the items of learning," said Gregory Bateson, "and you necessarily destroy all quality." That education can be only as strong as the links that bind its manifold subjects together need not be elaborately urged. At issue is not so much the success of departments in teaching their various disciplines as with the meaning of education as a whole. In schools and colleges alike we have been satisfied to talk about the importance of education without coming to terms with its meaning. We expect students to be motivated, to achieve the goals we set for them, to learn for the sake of learning. They must pass English, social studies, science, and mathematics; they must learn a foreign language. Yet in the end we leave them to deduce the meaning of all this activity for themselves, as if its value were self-evident.

Because schools and colleges are structured chiefly to specialize rather than to generalize knowledge, learning gets divided rather than integrated. Teachers trained as specialists naturally find it difficult to perceive patterns other than those within their own disciplines. Hermetically sealed inside their classrooms, they become increasingly isolated from their colleagues who live in different rooms and inhabit different segments of education. Only the students travel from room to room, sampling the parts but never the whole.

For as long as most of us can remember, the pattern that connects the items of learning in schools has been broken and the quality of education has correspondingly suffered. Withal, we find occasional attempts to bridge the various disciplines. Not infrequently, English is combined with history to provide a context for the former and a second voice for the latter. Then, too, there are humanities courses in which several of the arts are combined; e.g., music, art, literature, history. While such instances make a beginning at weaving together certain strands of learning, they are essentially multidisciplinary rather than interdisciplinary. Our chances of discovering the patterns that connect are destined to remain obscure until we can construct a working definition of interdisciplinary inquiry.

Let us therefore clarify the notion of interdisciplinary by stipulating that it involves not one thing but several, operating on four sequential levels of understanding that we may term *replication, historical association, correlation,* and *coalescence,* each of which in turn requires a brief explanation.

Level 1: Replication

At the level of replication, instruction usually juxtaposes subject matter belonging to established disciplines, much as we find in the curricular structure of every school where disciplines are taught side by side, but where the relations among these disciplines remain largely implicit. Interdisciplinary study at level I attempts to replicate in miniature the disciplinary structure found at large. This is achieved by extracting pieces of subject matter and placing them in some kind of sequence that implies a connection. In humanities courses, for example, we find some art, some literature, some history, or some music pieced together in a kind of mosaic that enables students to view smaller parts in terms of a larger whole. Usually, however, the parts imported from existing disciplines remain intact, unchanged by the composite into which they have been inserted.

Level 2: Historical Association

Level 2 constitutes what seems to us the next logical step in interdisciplinary inquiry. Here the pieces of subject matter become ordered in time. History becomes the "glue" that holds together the mosaic wherein ideas are seen as events, each of which is preceded, accompanied, or followed by other events. How and when something happens thus partially explains *why* it happens. We might infer, for example, that Cartesian philosophy with its mechanistic view of mind might naturally precede Newtonian physics that saw the world as mechanism acted upon by predictable forces. Time therefore becomes the ubiquitous and inevitable connector. Since everything must occur in time, history offers a ready vehicle for understanding our place in it, a way to construct a story from the world's infinite array of disparate events. Little wonder, then, that history most often defines the connections we discern among our multiple intellectual pursuits and that it so frequently serves as the backbone of the humanities.

Level 3: Correlation

While one may fashion a history of nearly any pursuit, it does not cut so evenly across the disciplines, especially those that inquire into the nature of intricate systems, such as language, logic, mathematics, or science. Though all of these subjects possess a history, their histories cannot begin to convey an adequate understanding of their content. To comprehend the nature of these disciplines we must move to another level, a level that will enable us to view their content from another perspective. Here the connections must be made more explicit, since the relationships involved tend to be more structural, functional, causal, recursive, reciprocal, and so forth. How, for example, might we compare language, music, and mathematics? Why is it that we can multiply a number but not a name? To answer these kinds of questions it is no longer sufficient to exhibit data and thread it with history. We must rely on our cumulative knowledge while at the same time finding ways to render that knowledge more accessible. Indeed, we must begin to understand something about the nature of understanding itself if we expect to penetrate this level.

Level 4: Coalescence

The fourth and final level of inquiry would deal primarily in relationships and meta-relationships. It would operate almost exclusively on the theoretical plane, its subject matter being the mind itself and the nature of intelligence, which are the seat of what we mean by interdisciplinary. Theories of mind attempt to coalesce all subject matter into a single unifying process, so that our understanding of time and space, number and causality, perception and creation fall under a uniform explanation. For this reason Level 4 represents an ideal towards which we may strive but not hope to capture and contain.

Having delineated these four levels of interdisciplinary inquiry, our rationale for an interdisciplinary course becomes clear. To some extent the four levels reflect the progress of inquiry in every discipline where one begins with the concrete and moves towards progressively more adequate explanations of the phenomena in question. In arithmetic, for example, we begin by learning a seemingly unconnected series of operations performed on apples and oranges—addition, subtraction, multiplication, division. Later on we learn how these operations are related; e.g., that multiplication is a recursive form of addition, that addition is the reciprocal of subtraction, and so forth. In algebra we come to understand that operations can exist independent of numerals, just as theorems in Euclidean geometry apply to an inexhaustible variety of triangles. Still further, we learn operations that may be performed on operations, and so on.

The difference between *intra*disciplinary and *inter*disciplinary inquiry appears to be largely a matter of latitude and level. Understanding any or all disciplines is not solely a matter of climbing the scale nor of choosing to occupy one level at the exclusion of others. It is a matter of *knowing* the scale and being able to traverse it, however tenuously. For the purpose of a course we can define student progress as combined growth in the latitude and level of understanding of a specified domain of study. By "latitude" we would mean the breadth or inclusiveness of content that falls within the given domain. By "level" we would mean the degree of correlation that is perceived among the items of content within that designated domain, however narrow or broad. If we were to designate level by a vertical axis and latitude by a horizontal axis, then a line bisecting the vertical and horizontal at a forty-five degree angle would indicate the ideal goal of interdisciplinary study.

The particular items of content do not especially matter except insofar as they not only permit but also encourage growth in both latitude and level. In "The Mind's Eye," a team taught, senior interdisciplinary course developed at Brookline High School, we created four units of inquiry: mathematics and metaphor, stories in space and time, culture and creativity, and the concept of consciousness. As with all curricular innovations, our initial efforts in The Mind's Eye were characterized by uncertainty and unevenness. In successive trials, however, the course began to take on a life of its own so that teachers and students alike began to see relationships that at first were only suspected. Here, for example is an excerpt from one student's final paper.

> The material is not a completely new and never before encountered subject; it is familiar things like physics and math and English. It is the way these subjects are taught that makes the course so unorthodox. To begin with, the three subjects are more often than not mushed together, so that it is entirely possible to

leap, in one breath, from quantum theory to character motivation in fiction and still make a completely coherent connection between the two. The only true divisions in the course are the class period's beginning and end.

And here is what our mathematics teacher had to say.

> Speaking for myself, the work we did helped me in the way I would most wish it would help our students: it pushed me toward the discovery of and commitment to an intellectual framework within which my truest perceptions could find a home.

"Clearly something is missing in the way we are educating our children," according to Frederick Turner. "And despite our penchant for administrative and financial solutions, I believe we must look to the *content* of education—its conception of the shape of the world, and therefore its manner of introducing students to it—for both a diagnosis and a cure." Fundamentally, says Turner, this missing something is "a sense of cognitive unity, a unity which imparts meaning to the world and from which our values unfold. We cannot go backward to look for this unity; but perhaps it lies before us if only we can cleanse the gates of our perception." (Turner, 1986, p.47)

Our gates of perception cleanse exceedingly slow, for the unity that Turner seeks lies latent within the subjects taught in every school. They are the patterns that connect the items of learning and that grant to this learning the meaning it has always promised but has yet to deliver.

The XYZ's of Grammar

When we speak of grammar, we refer not to one thing but to many. Yet when we teach grammar, we often convey the impression that it is a governing body of knowledge that can not only be known but also mastered. My worry is that, quite apart from knowing it, students are given no way to think about it, no framework in which to contemplate its nature or its use. When I ask a class what grammar is, I receive nearly as many answers as there are students. Grammar, they say, is the way to speak and to write correctly, the collection of rules for proper use of language, the explanation of how language works, a set of formulae for constructing good sentences. Despite the disparity among these definitions, the abiding impression is that this something called grammar constitutes a singular and circumscribed body of knowledge that one either knows or doesn't know. And if we were to ask the parents of these students the same question, chances are we would arrive at the very same impression.

At issue are whole generations that have, in my humble opinion, been misled, generations who sit on school committees, citizen input committees, and the PTO's. My interest in addressing this issue is thus a long-term project, its object being to educate the students who will be tomorrow's parents and will therefore exercise considerable influence on what is to be taught.

For a beginning, we need to distinguish between grammar and usage, which are commonly interpreted as the same thing. In the dictionary, in fact, we find them distinguished only as different interpretations of grammar; e.g., "the study of language as a systematically composed body of words that exhibit discernible regularity of structure (morphology) and arrangement into sentences (syntax), sometimes including the aspects of language as the pronunciation of words (phonology)." Usage, on the other hand, is defined as "a normative or prescriptive system setting forth the current standard of usage for pedagogical or reference purposes." Although there is a grammatical explanation for saying "It is I," I being the predicate nominative, as a matter of usage nearly everybody says, "It's me." One may acquire correct usage without knowledge of grammar. Usage relies on custom and convention, whereas grammar emanates from a more systematic source to which we now turn.

Think of grammar, then, not as one thing but essentially three: the *theory*, the *study*, and the *facility* of language; respectively Grammar X, Grammar Y, and Grammar Z, each of which remain separate and distinct. When we speak of the theory of language (Grammar X), we refer to different hypotheses for explaining how language works, each of which asks a particular kind of question that in turn yields a particular kind of answer. For the purposes of illustration, I choose three different theories of grammar: the functional, the structural, and the transformational or generative. Constructed in different eras, each of these theories bears the mark of its time and the preoccupations of the age in which it emerged. And each is designed to answer a carefully constructed question.

Functional grammar, for instance, which is the grammar most commonly studied in schools, asks "What are the names for the kinds of words and the forms in sentences which must be used in order to speak and write a language?"(Jesperson) What this question yields is principally a taxonomy, a classification of words and forms according to the functions they purportedly serve; e.g., the "parts of speech;" A noun is a person, place, thing, or idea. The oldest of the three theories, functional grammar emanated from the historical and descriptive preoccupations of the 19th century linguistic inquiry that sought to reconstruct Proto-Indo-European language.

Structural grammar, which arose primarily from attempts by anthropologists and linguists to record and classify Amer-Indian languages, asks a very different kind of question, namely, "What are the devices in language that signal structural meanings?"(Hockett) By structural meanings linguists of the early 20th century sought to discover not names but *frames* that apply to meaning. In other words, instead of defining a noun as a person, place, or thing, structural grammar determines that in English a noun is any word that can be substituted in the frame "The _____ was good." (Fries) Since most of the world's languages are not written, the task of the linguist is to describe language as it is spoken, not to prescribe how it should be written. The famous example used in structural grammar is Lewis Carroll's "Jabberwocky," whose nonsense words can nonetheless be identified as parts of speech according to the syntactical frames in which they appear. "The slithy toves," for example, are clearly an adjective and a plural noun.

Finally, at the onset of the computer age, **generative** grammar sought to answer the question, "What does a speaker know about the phonological and syntactic structure of his language which enables him to use and understand any of its sentences, including those he has never previously heard?" (Jacobs) In other words, how does a speaker make infinite use of finite means? The famous sentence arising out of this theory is "Colorless green ideas sleep furiously," a sentence that in all probability has never been said before and that makes no sense, yet is nonetheless acceptable grammatically. It is the "deep structure" of grammar that enables us to generate such a sentence.

In class, once I have framed and explained these questions, I point out that, being theories, none of these grammars is either complete or "correct." They are simply hypotheses about the nature of language that seek to answer a particular kind of question. What is of interest to the linguists is the process of inquiry they are constructing and the answers it yields. No linguist or grammarian has ever succeeded in describing the whole of any language, nor is any likely to, since language is the most complex system yet devised. According to perhaps our greatest American linguist, Edward Sapir, "Language is a mountainous and anonymous work of unconscious generations." It is also he who said, "All grammars leak."

So much for Grammar X, the theory of language. What, then, of Grammar Y, the study of language? Unlike Grammar X, Grammar Y is not an original inquiry into the nature of language. It is rather the explanatory form of Grammar X that presents the answers that the theory has already produced. Grammar Y thus retraces the steps of Grammar X much as the study of physics recapitulates the steps of Newton and Einstein, not with a view to constructing an original theory, but with the object of understanding an established theory, a theory in which the questions and answers are already implicit. The most common form of Grammar Y used in schools today is functional rather than structural or generative, both of which suffered controversial and fleeting trials in schools and have long since disappeared from classrooms.

This brings us to Grammar Z, the facility of language. Like Grammar Y, Grammar Z is learned, but unlike Y, grammar Z is never taught. Grammar Z comprises the rules that each of us unconsciously constructs in the course of learning our native tongue. It is the grammar that every speaker knows, the grammar every theory tries to construct, and the grammar that every study purports to explain. It is the construction of Grammar Z that prompts us to admire the child between two and five as "the hardest mental toiler on earth." (Chukovsky). Children individually and systematically construct their own grammars. For instance, a child will say things it has never heard, like "He goed to the store," because it is regularizing formation of the past tense in English, rather than using the strong version of the word to go—"went," which children often use before they will say "goed."

It has rightly been said that "if we taught children to speak, they would never learn." (Holt) The reason they would never learn is that grammars X, Y, and Z can in no useful sense be considered equivalent. The grammar we study, whichever one it may be, is neither theory nor facility, neither theoretical activity nor the mental configuration of the way in which we acquire language. Conversely, having facility for speech does not automatically enable us to engage in theoretical inquiry about language, for while all theories originate with questions, not all questions originate theories. Finally, not all theories are equally accessible to study or instruction, however sound and insightful such theories may be, as confirmed by the survival of the functional rather than the structural or generative in schools.

But, my students will ask, if the Grammars X, Y, and Z all differ, and neither the theory nor the study of language can unlock the mysteries of our facility, why study grammar? One may answer "Because it is there," "Because it is yours," or simply with another question, "Why not?" Yet here I am fond of quoting Oliver Wendell Holmes who was given to observe that "although certainty is generally an illusion, repose is not the end of man."

The Ozymandian Cycle

I t was Ozymandias, ancient king of kings in Shelley's famous poem, who had engraved upon his colossal statue the infamous phrase, "Look on my works, ye Mighty, and despair." Now all that remains of his once glorious empire is a shattered visage that lies at the feet of two vast and trunkless legs of stone standing alone in the desert. As the poet makes clear, Ozymandias is destined to be remembered not for his works but for the irony of his words stamped upon lifeless and forgotten things.

In assessing the events of the past few decades, we find the landscape of education similarly strewn with relics that have suffered a far speedier demise. These works are our curricula, the sculptures of learning that have been variously erected as monuments to passing preoccupations. See here the earthworks of science thrown up to stem the intrusion of Sputnik in the late fifties. And here stands the battered shrine erected in the name of creativity by those who firmly believed in the natural inclination of the child to learn—a work of the troubled sixties when Vietnamese villages burned, American cities smoldered, and schools seethed with unrest. Over here lingers a veritable ghost town that sprang up in the seventies to celebrate the age of alternatives in education. See there the storefront school, there the open "student-centered" classroom, here the bed of mainstreaming, and on the outskirts the shanties of electives. And look now at this monolith of the eighties, dedicated to "The Basics" and carved from the debris left by falling SAT's, plummeting enrollments, tax eruptions, high winds of inflation, and the siltings of recession. Lastly, as we enter the nineties, crossing the shifting dunes of phonics and whole language, we stand looking up at the pyramid of Accountability, at the top of whose terraced slopes waves the banner of Choice, which is in turn illuminated by the Beacon of Learning that casts its blinding shaft for all to plainly see.

On surveying the wreckage of our past endeavors, we find cause enough for despair. Gone are the halcyon days of limitless funding and manifold programs; gone, too, the commanding belief in the power of teachers and curriculum to change the course of events or the quality of human relations. Curriculum "has been tried" and its results found wanting. Today, education languishes, its recent innovations condemned, its coffers depleted, its veteran and beleaguered staff diminished, its facilities in disrepair, its students unprepared, its prospects decidedly dim.

Withal, education will somehow survive and no doubt prevail once again in a form as yet unrealized. However arid and grim the landscape, the Ozymandian cycle shall grind inexorably on. At long and shiny tables even now experts huddle to design some new edifice, while on lofty peaks and distant shores itinerant gurus gather round their disciples to contemplate our future. And one day soon the new preoccupation shall be upon us, sweeping in from some unexpected quarter to fill the present void. With it will arrive the fiery young zealots whose untried energies will quickly subdue all resistance and leave us quietly shaking our weary heads as we pass in the halls. Yet another monument will be raised, and if history has its way, this, too, will crumble and eventually fall, leaving its proponents standing spent amid their erstwhile fancies.

Like Ozymandias, our works are fleeting and our hopes ironic, for they appear to have little lasting impact on the character or quality of instruction. In a study of high school classrooms, Larry Cuban once found that despite two major reform movements in the course of the last century, "The overall picture of high school teaching since 1900 is striking in its uniformity: persistence of whole-group instruction, teacher talk outdistancing student, question/answer format drawn largely from textbooks, and little student movement in academic classes." (Cuban, 1982.) He concluded that the American high school, having survived four score years virtually unchanged, is not only "resilient," but also "remarkably invulnerable." While such persistence in the face of rampant flux has undeniable appeal, it must also give us pause to consider the evident disparity between what we think we are doing and what we are actually doing in schools. Had it been our intent to remain implacable and intransigent in the face of change, that would be one thing, but my impression is that schools today pride themselves on being responsive to the concerns of the communities they serve. How is it, then, that schools manage to remain "remarkably invulnerable"?

The answer in part lies in the way that curriculum is conceived. Traditionally, it is conceived as "something to teach," a course of study. On occasion this will entail a change of method, such as the open classroom where walls were pulled down and "individualized instruction" installed, but as a rule it focuses on subject matter—what shall be read, what concepts taught, what skills learned, what tests prescribed. So conceived, the manner in which curriculum is ordinarily produced in schools proves revealing. Typically, it will come prepackaged in the form of a text selected by some committee and handed down to the teacher. Alternatively, under the urge of fashion or the press of circumstance, teachers will be hired to develop curricula over a few weeks in early summer. Devoting the first few days to brainstorming, they set about selecting the appropriate readings and generating the required number of lessons, replete with behavioral objectives, exercises, assignments, student activities, measures of learning, and "suggestions for teaching." Writing furiously to meet the imposed deadline, they deliver reams of unformatted material before rushing off to recuperate. In the dog days of August these materials are deciphered with varying degrees of success, run off, collated and usually delivered after the start of school, at which time all teachers of the designated course are enjoined to follow the curriculum closely, so that its results can be evaluated and duly reported to those responsible for the expenditures involved. The resultant reports tend to be uniformly enthusiastic, thereby ensuring cheerful funding of additional workshops the following June.

That curriculum produced in this way can be installed without significantly altering the character of teaching or learning should come as no surprise. The wonder is not that much of it fails and conveniently disappears, but that any of it succeeds, much less survives. Where it survives it does so not because it improves teaching but because it is improved *by* teachers who must draw upon their own energy and resourcefulness to make it work. Unfortunately, these individual contributions seldom become an official part of the curriculum. Like a hot air balloon, it stays aloft only as long as individuals are willing to breathe life into it, but invariably collapses as soon as it changes hands.

At issue, however, is not so much the design or even the execution of curriculum but a simpler and deeper mistake. Like Ozymandias we tend to treat works as ends in themselves. We assume that instruction is governed by content and that by changing this content we can bring about changes in schools. But if eighty odd years of curriculum development and reform have failed to alter the character of instruction, as Professor Cuban has averred, then it appears that curriculum as traditionally conceived does not and really cannot bring about the changes we envision.

To understand why this is so, consider for a moment an analogous human activity more ancient and complex than even education—language. Changes in language are most readily apparent in vocabulary that is subject to the surge of argot and the swell of slang. One cannot learn a language merely by memorizing its words nor need one know all its words in order to speak a language fluently. At once our most unstable and expendable units of speech, words operate at the surface of language. Although we can create new words with abandon or shift and expand the meanings of old words, our language retains the indelible character of English.

Patterns of usage, on the other hand, comprise a deeper stratum of language. We are less aware of our manner of speaking than we are of the words we speak. We have to be taught to say, "It is I" and "Just between you and me" because usage becomes habitual and is therefore more resistant to change. Parents must struggle to teach their children to say "please" and "thank you," "hello" and "good-bye." Teachers must labor to expunge use of the ubiquitous "like" and "you know?" Our accents and expressions stick with us, often for life, and we are comfortable only with those who speak as we do.

Deeper still is the grammar or structure of language, so deep that although we must know this grammar in order to speak, we do not know it explicitly and must be taught how to bring it to the surface. The difficulty of acquiring this skill is familiar to every school child and the difficulty of teaching it familiar to every teacher. It is this depth that preserves grammar from change and renders it the most stable aspect of language. Our adjectives precede our nouns, our objects follow our verbs, our declensions for person and number, mood and tense are fixed. Though we can readily acquire vocabulary throughout our lives and more gradually adopt different habits of usage, our grammar remains fundamentally the same. It is the "software" of our language, its operating system, which we are not at liberty to alter.

Edward Sapir has characterized language as "a mountainous and anonymous work of unconscious generations." Of interest to us is the design of this ancient and venerable system. Changes in language occur most frequently at those levels that are most accessible but least important to the system as a whole. Thus, we are free to create words as much as we like only because they make the least difference: we can use them or reject them whenever we like. But the system is also designed so that those aspects that change the least can nevertheless accommodate those that change the most. This is why a stable and relatively fixed grammar can support an inexhaustible variety of words and sentences.

LANGUAGE	CURRICULUM
Vocabulary	Content
Usage	Method
Grammar	Structure

Now we are ready to return to curriculum. Curriculum is like language inasmuch as both are multileveled. Like vocabulary in language, content in curriculum is at once the most evident and most accessible aspect of instruction, hence, most often subject to change. Altering one's method of teaching, however, is like trying to alter one's customary usage of English, since both rely more on habit and performance than on deliberation. Methodology in curriculum is therefore more difficult to change, hence more controversial. We can teach Asian or European history, *The Red Badge of Courage* or *Huckleberry Finn* without breaking stride, but teaching the IMP math, Harvard Project Physics, or whole language requires a shift in both content and method.

So far, then, the analogy seems to hold: curriculum is like language inasmuch as content is like vocabulary and method is like usage. But how would we characterize the structure of curriculum? If the answer momentarily eludes us, perhaps this is because the structure of curriculum, like the grammar of language, constitutes the least accessible aspect of instruction. Just as we can learn to speak a language without any conscious knowledge of its grammatical structure, so too can we learn to teach without explicit awareness of what shapes our instruction. But our real difficulty in determining the structure of curriculum stems from what appears to be a contradiction, namely, that curriculum is structured according to content that we divide into disciplines or departments. In other words, we conceive curriculum to be structured according to its surface characteristics that are its most accessible yet least stable aspects. Think of it this way.

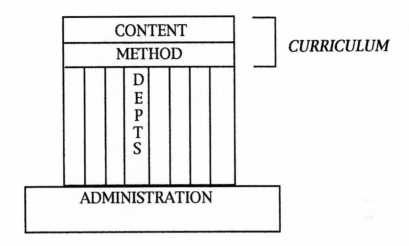

Here curriculum stands upon a single pillar, in this instance the departments, which are all similarly constituted and which offer the only means of instruction. These departments, in turn, are supported by the administration, which consists of houses, guidance, and the administration proper—the principal, assistant principals, and so on. Changes that affect curriculum occur almost exclusively at the topmost level of content and upon occasion at the secondary level of method. But the organization of instruction into departments, together with its administrative support, is not viewed as a part of the curriculum *per se.* Only content and occasionally method are considered relevant to instruction.

Now we are ready to define structure. *Curricular structure is the manner in which instruction is conceived, organized, prepared, and delivered.* Viewed in this way it is easy enough to see how schools have remained "remarkably invulnerable" to change. They have focused all their energies on the most accessible yet least important aspect of instruction—content, leaving the supporting structure of departments and administration virtually untouched. No one doubts, of course, that curriculum must include content, just as language must include words, or mathematics numbers. But to insist that instruction be governed by content alone is to invoke the Ozymandian cycle earlier described. Being most accessible, content appears to offer endless opportunities for innovation. This year we can offer a course in "Cowboys and Indians," "Your Checkbook," "Martian Manners," and "The Broadway Musical." Next year we can teach "The Noun," "Fractions," "The American Way," and "Employment." And for each of these subjects we can dutifully itemize goals and objectives, enumerate appropriate skills, stipulate modes of evaluation. But such possibilities are limitless only because the underlying conception of curriculum upon which they are based is correspondingly meager.

If we truly wished to alter our language, our best bet would be to alter its grammar, since the grammar affects vocabulary and usage while itself remaining perfectly stable. Let us say that from now on all adjectives will follow the nouns they modify and that number and tense will occur as prefixes instead of suffixes. That would be a change. Similarly, a more comprehensive view of curriculum would not only include its underlying structure but would also seek to broaden and diversify that structure. Thus, in place of our present monolithic structure, we might divide that structure among five "pillars" of instruction.

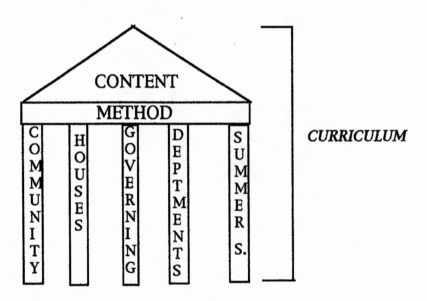

Each of these five pillars of instruction would be distinguished by its special mix of content, method, and organization. The departments, for instance, would continue to focus on traditional areas of content as before, but they would no longer claim instruction as their exclusive domain. Houses might undertake instruction of a more holistic and interdisciplinary nature, as would befit the heterogeneous constituency they serve. They could offer regularly scheduled tutorials that would meet in place of homeroom. In contrast, adult and community education could join this structure by specializing in topics and issues of both practical and continuing concern—matters belonging more to lifelong education than to the standard fare of schooling. At the same time, a summer school could offer what amounted to a third semester of special opportunities in intensive, extensive, experimental, and enrichment learning. Finally, the administration might assume responsibility for instruction in governance, planning, decision-making, and leadership. Together these five pillars would offer a flexible though integrated use of resources that are already in place in most schools, thus providing the kind of diversity that teaching and learning require but currently lack.

Of Ozymandias, king of kings, Shelley tells us that,

> Nothing beside remains. Round the decay
> Of that colossal wreck, boundless and bare
> The lone and level sands stretch far away.

Something beside must remain. The content of instruction must be rooted in structure. By structure we mean, in essence, the school—a community designed for and devoted to the production of learning. Structure is the means by which learning is created, supported, and delivered. Learning includes not only what there is to be learned, but also how that gets decided and implemented. It is the policies and facilities, the organization and administration, the shape and the context upon which learning must ultimately depend. To view it as anything less is to diminish and sadly underrate the task of teaching and learning, to defer to the mighty at the expense of the meek.

Axioms of Education[6]

For those who serve at the forefront of education certain axioms are in force that, though unknown to non-professionals, nonetheless guide the conduct of academic affairs. I call them axioms because their truth is so self-evident that in the ordinary course of events we mistake them for common sense, assuming that our adversaries will appreciate the futility of questioning our premises. In these times of reform, however, perhaps it is advisable to air these axioms so that the general public will come to see the reasonableness of our cause and grant us their generous support. I list them here in no special order or priority, since in principle they are all equally sound and may thus be happily applied to nearly any circumstance that falls within their purview.

Axiom 1. Academic standards rise in inverse proportion to the number of students allowed to reach them.

Amid all the talk of academic excellence these days, there is consternation in schools about how best to achieve it. One strategy has been to make grading more rigorous and thus put a stop to the epidemic of A's and B's now being awarded to students. That we shall be able to raise academic standards by reducing the number of students allowed to reach them seems at first a dubious proposition. Since more students will ostensibly be doing less well, it is difficult to imagine our claiming that they are actually doing better merely because the standards are higher. Thus, when Johnny or Jane comes home with a report card crowded with C's and D's instead of the usual A's and B's, their parents' reactions are likely to be unfavorable.

In these matters, however, we must not be unduly alarmed by surface phenomena. The measure of our standards lies not in the grades themselves but in their comparative worth. Since the worth of a C will approximately equal that of our present B, what we will have actually done is to increase the value of the C, albeit still "lower" than the prior B. In reality, therefore, the C will be worth more than the prior B, because though it is of equivalent value it will signify a comparatively greater *yield*. Whereas before we had to award a B to represent the level of excellence, now we can get the very same value for *less*. In this sense, raising academic standards is not only beneficial to our nation's youth, spurring them on to greater heights of achievement; it is also a real bargain.

Axiom 2. The quality of education is directly proportional to the quantity of information acquired.

Children need to learn more than they think they do. The lessons of the past few decades have taught us that the child's natural inclination to learn is insufficient for achieving an adequate education. Students are in no position to judge what they need to learn until they already know it. Only then can they decide.

To improve the quality of education we must therefore raise the number of requirements needed for graduation. And for each of these requirements we must increase the amount of information that children are asked to absorb. Too many children today have no idea where Sri Lanka or the Palmer Peninsula is. Too few have ever heard of "carrying coals to Newcastle," Mary Cassatt, Charon, chordates, Clementine, curriculum vitae, cytoplasm—and that's just a sampling from the C's.

The question is not how many students are dropping out of school today, but how little information they are dropping out with. Our dropouts either need to be more literate or to have a better reason for dropping out. By increasing requirements and the amount of information that each entails, we provide this reason because then they will learn, or at least suspect, how little they actually know. In this way failure can be better quantified and success authenticated. Best of all, once the requisite information has been acquired, it can be shared, and the children of tomorrow need never worry about having something to talk about.

Axiom 3. If some portion of content cannot be taught successfully at a given level, start teaching it earlier.

We are all aware of the crucial role that practice plays in learning. When children fail to assimilate some concept or batch of information, it is usually because they lack confidence. Like the rest of us, they fear the unknown. In these instances our wisest course is to dilute the material in question and start them thinking about it sooner. Our strategy is to accustom them to the material, making it an integral part of their daily lives. Take Boyle's Law, for instance—a favorite of so many physics teachers. On the face of it, this is a perfectly transparent concept: the pressure of a given quantity of gas varies inversely with its volume at constant temperature, or to be more precise, $pv = k$. That children have difficulty understanding this concept is through no fault of their own. After all, few if any actually know who Boyle is, or was. They quite naturally assume that this law has something to do with infection.

Very well, then: our first task is to introduce Mr. Boyle so that he is more than just a name. In middle school every class can prominently display a picture of Boyle, suitably framed and inscribed. It can say, "Bob Boyle, The Gas Man, 1662," or something equally apt that will convey that here we have not just a law but a real human being. Children will get to know Bob Boyle as a person, a familiar face that will become part of the furniture of young minds.

But that's just for starters. Connecting names with faces is undoubtedly of estimable benefit, yet we know that if learning is to take root and grow it must become dynamic, an active and integral part of our lived experience. What we need, therefore, are *hands on* activities, a chance for children to manipulate concepts in concrete terms. These can be inserted at any point in the elementary curriculum.

The plan, however, is this: if children are expected to understand Boyle's Law in high school, they must be given the opportunity to play with gases as a part of their normal activity. Because of the safety factor of which we must always be aware, I would suggest that they begin with helium and work their way up. For the environmentally minded, we can employ balloons heated with solar energy. For this, history buffs can use goatskins and magnifying glasses. Teachers should be encouraged to use their creative talents in these matters; the important thing is to have pupils heat gas and observe what happens.

This is our "proactive" stance and just one more example of how to make science live. The real value of our approach, however, lies in its broad applicability. Think of the Council of Trent, the importation of flax, fractions, Mayan glyphs, iambic pentameter, grammar! It goes without saying that once this axiom is rigorously applied across the curriculum, the wonderful world of learning can be a better place in which to live.

Axiom 4. If some portion of content can be taught successfully, find some way to teach it faster.

In schools, time is of the essence. There is so much to learn and to teach that we must always be cognizant of how effective our teaching actually is. Today, we hear a great deal about "time on task." The astonishing efficiency of our Asian brothers and sisters is but one case in point. If the number of Toyotas plying our highways is any indication, we are falling drastically behind in our production of learning.

Our course is therefore clear. If we cannot extend the hours that our children spend in school, we can at least try to make the best possible use of those hours that they are with us. This can be accomplished in a number of ways. In my travels around the nation's schools, I have been struck by how slowly our teachers seem to talk. Pick up any World War II movie at your local video store—"Tora, Tora, Tora," for example—and you will see what I mean. Notice how the Japanese clip their words? Those pilots talk so fast you can hardly understand them. True enough, they are really just actors, but this does not mitigate my point. Put a Japanese teacher in one room and an American teacher in another and have them teach exactly the same lesson. By the time the American gets through reading the roll, the Japanese teacher will be halfway through the lesson. The same goes for rap singers versus, say, Bing Crosby.

Recent research and technology has shown that our minds can process information much faster that we can communicate it. On a variable speed tape recorder running at twice the speed we can still understand what is being said. And so can our children! Were our teachers to increase their average rate of speech by a mere 10%, our children could increase their knowledge proportionately.

Axiom 5. Educational excellence is directly proportional to the amount of effort expended.

Schools in need of reform simply need to try harder. After all, these are human institutions and as such require harsh incentives to keep them in line. Think about taxes, for example. Would anyone consider paying taxes if there were not strict penalties for not doing so? Certainly not. Well, the same applies to schools. Those that fail to reach prescribed standards of excellence need to suffer the consequences of their inaction and take their medicine. It is incontrovertible that once a lesson has been taught, excuses for not learning it disappear, unless, of course, it hasn't been taught correctly or at all. Consequently, either the teacher or the students are at fault, possibly both. Those who fail to reach some degree of excellence therefore need to be punished, so that others may see that sloth does not pay and are thus encouraged to increase the energy and the seriousness with which they view their destinies. If we want our nation's education to improve, we need to be serious and stop fooling around. Bereft of dire consequences—firing teachers, locking school doors, army recruitment—our shoulders make no contact with the proverbial wheel.

Axiom 6. Only the classics should be read in school because some children may never want to read again.

As long as children are reading, they might as well read something worth remembering. The other day a mother thanked the good Lord that her oldest son had been forced to read every single word of *Silas Marner* and *Lorna Doone* when he was in school under the strict tutelage of Ms. Fidditch, because he hasn't read a single book since. We think that because great books are hard to read children will not like them. Whether they like them or not, they need to learn what real reading is. Otherwise, they will not be exposed to their cultural heritage, for unless the classics are read in school, chances are they won't be read at all. Witness how few people read *Silar Marner* and *Lorna Doone* today. Those who have missed this experience will probably never know what it is like and will thus be condemned to journey through life never fully literate.

Axiom 7. Neither the effectiveness nor the propriety of a school rule may be judged until it has been totally enforced.

When administrative policies in a school don't work, it is usually because some portion of the faculty or student body chooses to ignore them. That students should on occasion veer from the just and upright path is understandable. After all, they are young and do not as yet appreciate the necessity of conformity. We must remind ourselves that students are compelled to attend school because they are ignorant and slovenly in their habits. It is easy enough to claim innocence of intent once a law has been transgressed, but such is the nature of laws that they cannot be adhered to while remaining unknown. To those students who beg ignorance before the law, our answer is therefore clear: the purpose of school is to learn the law.

Unfortunately, there are always those clever members of staff who try to muddy the waters by claiming that "rules are made to be broken." To these we can answer that if nobody ever broke the rules, there wouldn't need to be any. Since everybody does break rules at one time or another, their existence cannot be questioned. From protracted experience we have learned that rules work only when the reason for breaking them is removed through uniform enforcement. To those who object to enforcing unnecessary rules, our answer is this: when rules are unnecessary, they require no effort to enforce because everybody is following them of their own accord. Such rules therefore persist at no cost to anybody and consequently cannot be singled out as cause for objection.

In conclusion, our advice to school administrators is essentially this: "If it doesn't work, enforce it."

Axiom 8. If everybody were allowed to do everything, nobody would get credit for doing anything.

Every generation operates under the assumption that it is unique. This is especially true of the current generation that believes itself exceptional, contrary to evidence. While sociological causes are always difficult to pin down, a generation raised with the Internet cannot long remain above suspicion. Having been catered to for most of their lives, today's students have managed to internalize a canon of unrealistic expectations about life's privileges. They are tenacious in their belief that rules and work are reserved for older people, and that if labor can be circumvented, youth claims first right of refusal.

This being the case, much of today's teaching is absorbed in matters of containment. The object of this instruction is to convince individuals that they belong to a class of people whose obligations exceed their rights. Central to this instruction is the cognizance that as soon as one rule is brooked all others are laid waste. To the dictum that "If I let you do this, everybody else will want to do it," the usual reply is that nobody else needs to know, or that the person who invents the exception gets to break the rule because where leaders are to be valued followers remain denied. Our argument takes the usual dictum a step further. In effect, we say, "If I let you do it, then it will no longer be worth doing because you will forfeit your uniqueness once others inevitably follow." Faced with the prospect of no longer being exceptional, they will willingly rejoin the herd.

> *Axiom 9. The best approach for reforming education is to mandate a test*
> *that assumes the reform is already in place, then count those who do*
> *not measure up.*

If we knew exactly what and how to teach, there would be no need for testing, so confident would we be of our content and method. Unfortunately, not all teachers know how to teach or students to learn. The only fair way to determine who is qualified to teach and which of their students reach an arbitrary level of knowledge is to create a test that everybody takes. Our assumption is that in the last analysis education is merely what standardized tests test. Tests must be standardized because not everybody knows how to make them. Were we to leave testing in the hands of individual schools, we would have no way of comparing one school with another, and consequently of knowing which schools to single out as "in need of improvement." By "improvement" we mean that in the best of all worlds, every school must be the same as every other, irrespective of race, class, gender, culture, geographical location, urban or rural, rich or poor, homogeneous or heterogeneous. After all, if we cannot tell who's behind, how can we know who's ahead? Or vice versa?

Whatever is known can be successfully tested. Whatever is not known is not worth worrying about.

THE PROFESSION

Just Teaching[7]

When upon occasion my students ask me why I teach, I tell them that it is so I will have someone to talk to. This retort provokes both surprise and dismay. Although their response is suitably measured, they are evidently distressed to discover that a figure of presumed learning and power should have to stoop to the likes of them for company, that so public a man could in private seem so solitary. No doubt they expect to hear how much I like kids, how I live to see their eyes alight with learning, or even how much I enjoy vacations. I tell them the truth instead, the truth that Dr. Samuel Johnson knew long ago.

> The life that is devoted to knowledge passes silently away, and is very little diversified by events. To talk in public, to think in solitude, to read and to hear, to inquire, and answer inquiries, is the business of the scholar. He wanders about the world without pomp or terror, and is neither known nor valued but by men like himself. (Preface to his Dictionary)

To talk in public, to think in solitude: here lies the essential disparity whose implications so few fully grasp. Wherever teaching occurs, or is likely to occur, there will be a public—the teacher and the student. They will gather in some room to pursue some purpose. And prior to this gathering the teacher will in solitude contemplate his purpose and determine how best to pursue it. For a time it appeared as if this venerable practice might be abrogated, the teacher supplanted by a machine, instruction "individualized" through the wonders of technology. The teacher would be effectively removed and the student left alone to learn "at his own pace." The increments of learning would be so reduced that the student could scarcely help but advance, reinforced by ineluctable rightnesses. Programmed to anticipate every alternative, these machines could be better prepared than the most enterprising teacher; their patience could not flag. And so it looked as if the problems of teaching had been resolved: teachers were freed from their oppressive burden of public exposure and private doubt.

Such expectations notwithstanding, teachers abide, their task little diversified by events, much as Johnson had earlier foreseen. At once still public and private, the life devoted to knowledge teeters upon a delicate balance. To teach is to sustain a gregarious insularity. Consider the public side. On the average teachers talk in public for five hours each day. In the course of a year's instruction, they will have been subjected to the protracted scrutiny of their students for a thousand hours. (How long might friendship, to say nothing of parenthood, withstand the rigors of such intensive interaction? Talk to your friends or children for an hour each day. Make your talk interesting as well as informative. Give them something to do while you are gone. Assess their progress; report to their guardians. Then watch their eyes alight with learning.)

Exposure of this sort naturally leaves hidden no quirk of speech or gesture, no article of dress nor habit of thought. Long after their lessons have faded into blessed obscurity, we can recall our teachers with uncanny clarity—their shoes and glasses, their giggles and glares, their gaffs and favors. We remember the ways in which we were taught rather than the actual content of that teaching. Our learning has been driven by those who have deigned to make public their person.

Consider now the persons made public. How do they decide what to teach? Presumably, they teach what they themselves have been taught— if not precisely, then in some combination. Once a workable formula has been concocted, it remains immutable, like a master cut that yields countless repetitions. To the outsider, in other words, teaching appears to require only initial training and occasional reminding. That at least was my own summary assessment when I undertook the task. Imagine my surprise when in an interview for my first job a venerable teacher— Tinker by name—delivered his opinion that it took five years to make an English teacher. At the time I thought this extravagant and quietly scoffed at one who would so magnify his labors. There were tricks to be sure— intriguing assignments, engaging topics for composition—but by and large the task amounted to amassing "materials"—lessons, units, tests. What's more, as I had learned in my methods courses, it would be trendy to punctuate instruction with "audio-visual techniques," which at the time comprised use of an overhead projector with colored overlays. I saw myself as the cool facilitator pictured even now in advertisements, pointer in hand, smiling benignly as I push the button for the next frame while an ecstatic throng looks on. And besides, the textbook publishers had seen to everything: the questions were in the back, the answers tucked into the yellow insert of the teacher editions, and the test on Friday. All one needed to be concerned about was "discipline."

But Tinker was right, indeed, optimistic. Once in the traces, every novice teacher discovers that irrespective of their training they are secretly incompetent. They find that teaching cannot be practiced like tennis—service, ground strokes, a little volleying. There are no practice students: you are either teaching them or you are not. Nor are there practice schools that can purport to represent real schools with their special communities, their children, their policies, their staff. Neither has a way been found to simulate the crushing pressure of daily exposure. Of course, beginning teachers fear the fault to be their own, however loudly they may complain about the programs that have seen fit to certify them in what they suddenly find themselves unqualified to execute. By the end of October, when they have expended units leisurely prepared for a methods course, they begin to understand the magnitude of the task so lightly undertaken. With Christmas light-years hence and the great maw of studentry clamoring for daily sustenance, they panic, laying waste their fields of knowledge, stuffing students with whatever materials they can find, scattering minds—as Robert Frost used to say—over taste and opinion.

Ultimately, we discover that to teach is to create, not to transmit. Schools drown in material, yet judge nothing quite suitable. And although we know that it is teachers who drive content rather than the reverse, we cling to the notion that somewhere the perfect lesson, book, or course lies wedged in rock, waiting to be pulled free. At professional conferences we haunt the booths, choking our plastic bags with promises. At department meetings we enter still another plea for greater communication, for new materials and techniques to share, for resource files, for visits to other schools, for educational paratroopers to drop in and distribute automatic ideas. All our days are Monday, all our nights Sunday. We cry for counsel, crave relief.

But there is no help save commiseration with those who know and share our plight. We must talk in public, think in solitude. We must teach ourselves: teach ourselves how to teach and how to learn, teach what we are and what we believe. Create! How else would we have it? It is the old dilemma voiced by the Grand Inquisitor: bread or freedom. If we wish to be fed instruction, we must accept its chains. If we want to be unfettered, we must embrace our terrible freedom and create.

These are the implications of the peculiar disparity between exposure and solitude that Johnson deemed endemic to a life devoted to knowledge, the fulcrum of that delicate balance upon which we teeter. One might well view the annals of education as a series of attempts to tamper with this balance. Of the much exalted age of classical education, it could be said that the balance favored the private aspect of teaching, allowing those with specialized knowledge of ancient languages to dictate the rigid course of learning. Latin and Greek had become private languages of the elite, effectively shielding education from public view. To talk Latin in public, as Harvard valedictorians do even today, and to study it in private was neither to inquire nor to answer inquiries of ostensible urgency. Little wonder that in those days scholars were unknown and unappreciated except by those like themselves. To outsiders, who then comprised virtually everyone, such talk was merely arcane display. This does not deny that much of value stood to be learned; it merely suggests that such learning became a relatively isolated affair.

Today, of course, the converse holds true. Perhaps to compensate for the tenor of the preceding age, we have become preoccupied with the public aspect of teaching. Teachers must now be held "accountable," content broken down into transparent "skills" whose acquisition may be conveniently verified. Individuality that persists in the form of understanding, enthusiasm, or wonder is now subject to suspicion, if only because it is "vague." To marvel, which for the Greeks was the beginning of knowledge, is to linger in the idle realms of romance, to loiter upon the threshold of precision, thus impeding the real business of education, namely, the advancement of skills and the attainment of articulated goals. Somehow learning has become identified with the amount of money needed to produce it. Education has waxed economical, being "data driven." In consequence, the business of the scholar is not to talk and to think, to read and to hear, or to inquire and answer inquiries; it is to *produce*. Nowadays, teachers are expected to produce something consumable rather than consuming.

It is time that teaching came of age, that its delicate balance be not only restored but also broadly affirmed. By teaching, I do not mean teachers alone, although they obviously figure centrally in the process. I mean the creation of knowledge in the mind of the learner and all that this entails. Teachers must be learners if anything of value is to be created. They must speak in public with the conviction that is derived from ownership and dredged from solitude. Similarly, students must be more than objects of learning, receptacles of knowledge. They must be partners in the creation, transformers of instruction into individual truths, consumed by learning rather than consumers of it. We need not apologize for the glowing idealism voiced in this conception; it is the aim of education to be ideal! If realism is our object, let us return to the fields and the boiler shops where facts abound.

We can begin by insisting on the centrality of teaching and the uniqueness of its task. We do not need to pretend that teachers are like doctors or novices like interns. We need not listen to those who would have us campaign for learning as if truth were seeking office and were subject to vote. Without pomp or terror, learning has clout only with those who pursue it. We need not succumb to the notion that schools resemble corporations and, consequently, that students are products to be efficiently produced or that teachers are shopkeepers whose accounts must be audited. Nor need we accede to the prevailing supposition that administrators are like officers and teachers their enlisted. To administer means to serve, not command. Those who work in schools but who do not teach feed upon teaching. A profession that accords highest status to those who do not practice its art leaves little to profess.

A profession is an avowal of faith. What are the articles or our faith and wherein lie their uniqueness? To begin with, as Johnson has suggested, teaching is a multifold activity, one that includes speaking, thinking, reading, listening, questioning, answering. Taken together, these activities constitute what we generally call "inquiry." This article bears repeating if only because of the enduring penchant for oversimplifying an extraordinarily complex process: to assume, for example, that teaching consists solely of performance in the classroom or of competence as measured by some test. Whereas classroom performance and competency tests may be indices of teaching, they can never presume to encompass it. Teachers perform inasmuch as they talk in public. They are competent insofar as they think in solitude. But they are effective only as far as they inquire. In teaching, readiness is all.

This brings us to our second article: inquiry must be individual before it can be collective. Subject matter does not exist apart from persons who know it, pursue it, and interpret it. To understand a subject is to understand how it fits into various minds, including one's own. Teachers wear their subjects, and students don them. Consequently, what a teacher has to teach is himself in the guise of a discipline, a single mind in the grip of a set of ideas. Standards refer to the tightness of that grip upon the teacher as well as the students. If we would measure a student's understanding of a poem or a theorem, let us take his pulse.

If teaching is, in effect, inquiry and inquiry is at bottom individual, our third article would be that inquiry is necessarily continuous and therefore cumulative. Learning is by nature insufficient: we are consumed by it to the degree that we detect its incompleteness. In teaching we therefore expect to learn; yet in schools, insofar as policies would admit, we are evidently expected to age but not to grow. Teachers bring their credentials with them, certifying them to teach a particular subject. If after three years of teaching their performance is judged satisfactory by various superiors, they are granted tenure. Thereafter, barring incidents of blatant insubordination, rank incompetence, or brazen immorality, their salaries automatically increase in set increments. Should they elect to acquire further credentials elsewhere, they are granted additional increments. However equitable this scheme may at first appear, it is an odd way in which to conduct an institution devoted to learning. Schools house teaching but do not themselves teach; they are purveyors of knowledge rather than perpetrators of it, teaching what is elsewhere learned yet nowhere else taught in the same manner.

Experience does not assure growth any more than seniority guarantees excellence. By relying on outside credentials, performance checks, and competency tests, schools effectively abdicate responsibility for educating their staff. In-service workshops qualify as token gestures, since they are inevitably designed to cut across disciplines (individual instruction, gifted and talented, human relations) or to amplify special concerns (career education, learning disabilities, drug abuse). Although such topics may enrich awareness of components in schooling, they diffuse rather than focus inquiry, offering variety instead of continuity, scope in place of depth, commonality in lieu of individuality, aggregation at the expense of development. Teachers who want to learn and to grow, who under extraordinary demands and pressures are trying to carve a life from learning, languish in the classroom. The only way they can move up is to move out, to attend institutions of "higher" learning or to escape to the sidelines of administration.

But we should be remiss were we to construe teaching as merely that which takes place in a class. However continuous, inquiry need not be confined, for in principle its contexts are limitless, its means diverse. Much of our best teaching is informal—a brief exchange in the hall, an extended dialogue after school, participation in sports, field trips. Again, however, schools assume a passive role in fostering such diversity. Teachers are paid, as they should be, for undertaking commitments beyond the classroom. Nevertheless, it is not considered part of a teacher's training and development to engage in so-called extracurricular activities with students. Instead, they are expected to attend workshops in human relations with colleagues.

Our final article of faith is perhaps the most encompassing. Besides being individual, continuous, and diverse, inquiry is universal. We teach for the world, not just for our communities, our students, or ourselves. Knowledge is meant to be shared. "Speak your latent conviction," said Emerson, "and it shall be the universal sense, for the inmost in due time becomes the outmost." Education is essentially an externalizing process, a gradual decentering of the self. As teachers we must strive to attain the outmost by way of the inmost, to speak in public what we think in solitude. And our public is no less than the universe, for such is the aim of all true inquiry.

These, then, are the articles of faith implicit in the view of teaching here espoused, articles that ultimately pertain to the manner in which we conduct education. We have said that the life devoted to knowledge pivots upon a delicate balance, a taut wire that links the public with the private aspects of teaching. Our view is that the enterprise of teaching is essentially one of inquiry, and that conduct of such inquiry must be at once individual, continuous, diverse, and universal if it is to flourish.

All very well, you say: we may think as we like, but how do we propose to act? It is once again Sunday and tomorrow we must stand before one hundred pairs of probing eyes.

Let us commence boldly then. We must take education in our own hands. Because teaching is an experience unlike any other, we must define that experience for ourselves and act accordingly. We must hold schools accountable for teaching. When a teacher is hired by a school system, it is incumbent upon that system to make its expectations plain. To demand unrelieved excellence from a teacher is not only unrealistic; it is also downright irresponsible. Are we to throw the teacher to the students and record in triplicate what happens? Are we to imagine that the salary schedule step list constitutes a personnel policy sufficient for guiding teachers through a lifetime of fruitful inquiry? Does the union contract include a career design plan worthy of the profession it claims to serve? In these days of declining enrollments, reduction in force, tax referenda, and inflation, what provisions are being made to ensure that teachers who survive can not only maintain but also improve prior standards? Finally, what promise does teaching presently hold for the next generation of teachers?

The outlook for education is admittedly bleak. Yet if we can profess faith in ourselves and in our pursuit, surely we can create a context in which that pursuit may prosper.

On the Excellence of Teaching[8]

E ducation is in the news again. We hear, almost daily, that the schools
have reached a new low, that they are inundated by "a rising tide of
mediocrity" that places our nation "at risk." According to one report the
professional life of teachers is "unacceptable." And by the reckoning of
another, the number of parents who said they would like to have their
children become teachers in public schools dropped from 75% in 1969
to 46% in 1981.

Such reports and opinions notwithstanding, the matter comes down to
this: the quality of education cannot surpass the quality of those who
educate. Whatever our funds and facilities, however we construe the
core of our curriculum or determine that its content has been learned,
the essence of education lies not in the *what* but the *who*. The future of
education rests squarely upon its teachers.

In the considered opinion of those who take it upon themselves to chart
the course of education, teachers can be paid more, their working
conditions improved, their professional training elevated, their careers
divided so that excellence and experience can advance in stepwise fashion
until they yield both enlarged responsibility and respectable
remuneration. The presumption seems to be that once these enlightened
policies are set in motion, teaching will take its place among the world's
prestigious pursuits, thus ultimately attracting the kind of talent it so
urgently needs and richly deserves.

Yet for all the good intentions and celebrated advice now issuing forth,
we know in our hearts that little of substance will emerge. After the
campaign speeches are made and the flood of reports written, the
urgency of our cause will quickly subside. Budgets will inevitably be

compromised and ambitious plans systematically pared until we are left with more to do but without the requisite means to do it. The changes wrought will be cosmetic and will shortly become indistinguishable from our present routine.

And when, as in times before, this current surge of reform gradually dissipates and fails to bring about significant or lasting change, we will drift into retirement blaming others for education's demise. In truth, however, we shall have only ourselves to blame, for once again we will have allowed others to determine what we, the teachers, actually know best. We will have yet again forfeited the right to determine the course of our careers. One might just as well try to improve medicine without consulting doctors, or regulate the law apart from legislators.

"There is in us a tendency," said Eric Hoffer, "to locate the shaping forces of our existence outside ourselves. Success and failure are unavoidably related in our minds with the state of things around us . . . The tendency to look for all causes outside ourselves persists even when it is clear that our state of being is a product of personal qualities." Similarly, the tendency to locate the shaping forces of education outside ourselves persists even when it is clear that the quality of teaching determines the quality of learning. We want to believe that the cause of teaching rests primarily in unity and numbers, that our influence must be felt in the corridors of power and high political office, even though it is plain that such expensive and distant strategies are ineffectual in resolving current ills.

Schools do not improve teaching; teaching improves schools. Structure schools as we may, contrive curriculum as we might, the power and thrust of learning ultimately depends on what teachers can make happen in the classroom. If we would change schools, then we must first change ourselves and the rest will follow. Blaming wages and working conditions, evaluation and supervision, curriculum and discipline is like blaming the dog's tail for not making him happy.

Perhaps this is the time when teaching at last can come of age. A profession that refuses to define itself and stipulate the criteria of its art leaves too little either to profess or to admire. The true irony of our predicament is that whereas teachers wield incredible power, they persist in behaving as if they were enslaved.

A Question of Merit

"**I**t is the fate of those who toil in the lower employments of life," said Samuel Johnson, "to be rather driven by fear of evil, than attracted by the prospect of good, to be disgraced by miscarriage, or punished for neglect, where success would have been without applause, and diligence without reward." Such was the lot of the hapless lexicographer, according to Johnson, whose endeavors were as unfamiliar to the eighteenth century as they have no doubt remained to the twenty-first. Yet his characterization captures the predicament so familiar to those who labor in the lower echelons of education, where today it has become the lot of the school teacher "to remove rubbish and clear obstructions from the paths of Learning and Genius, who press forward to conquest and glory, without bestowing a smile on the humble drudge that facilitates their progress."

That the lowly status of teachers might have some bearing on the quality of learning in our schools has been slow to dawn on those who take it upon themselves to chart the course of education. Not until the nation had been judged "at risk," its schools allegedly awash in "a tide of mediocrity," did reformers surmise that the fates of learning and of those who facilitate its progress were inextricably bound. And so began the raft of proposals calculated to elevate the profession: more stringent certification requirements would be demanded, teacher competency tests required; minimum salaries would be raised, schemes of merit pay instituted, career ladders installed. Once these measures were in place, teachers and teaching might together flourish and the rising tide that threatened them eventually recede.

Although these reforms fuel the hope that our maligned and beleaguered calling may one day assume its rightful place among the honored professions, the legions of humble drudges are not destined to become leagues of princely pedagogues by mere waves of the legislative wand.

Metamorphosis of the drudge calls for deeper measures. For now we see in the glass darkly what is manifest face to face: merit is but the mirror in which we behold a flat and silvered image of all that teaching implies. Like all specular images, however, it reflects only what lies at the surface.

Take the classroom. It goes without saying that a system of evaluation that failed to include classroom observation would be difficult to defend, much less imagine. But by the same token, what happens in a given set of classes cannot begin to encompass, much less represent, the merit that teaching demands. Teachers are like prophets who must daily wager all their experience against the vagaries and caprice of human minds. They must foresee what students are likely to know about a given topic, what obstacles they will encounter in understanding a concept, what questions they will ask, and what kinds of answers they must be given in order to advance their understanding. Telling examples must be invented, often on the spot, that will shake a concept suddenly free from the mire of conflicting preconceptions, lifting the veil of mystery like a curtain, and momentarily revealing the truth, naked and quivering.

If this is the ideal to which we aspire, it is also the result that we seldom capture. For before us sits an itchy and ragtag audience whose fickle moods are dictated by the time of day, the day of the week, the season of the year, and doubtless the phases of the moon. However innocent, they are marked with all the foibles that characterize human nature. Yet we take them as and when they come—angry or docile, alienated or inspired, compulsive or spoiled. Like aging performers before unaging patrons, we play out our lives in relentless segments, quietly celebrating our occasional triumphs, but dreading the inevitable lesson that begins to falter and then dies an unlamented death with twenty minutes still left in the period.

Those who view instruction from afar are fond of saying that teachers must be held accountable for what they do. In some instances accountability means results that students obtain on standardized tests. In others, it means a satisfactory score on a teacher's competency test. But for the most part accountability means that someone must be hired to watch what happens in classes and to judge the merit of the teacher's performance. As liquid assumes the shape of the container into which it is poured, so is the classroom thought to be a vessel in which learning conforms to whatever may be taught. To ensure this confirmation, the teacher designs a plan to yield the behaviors that are sought. "By the end of the lesson," the plan intones, "the students will know such-and-such to be the case, and that they know this will be evidenced by A, by B, or by C." In deciding the success of the lesson, one need only wait for A or B or C to emerge just as the teacher foretold. And in the event that they do not emerge, either the method by which they are sought or the aims themselves must be revised accordingly. It is upon such stark grounds that meritorious performance usually stands or falls.

At issue is how instruction can be calibrated so that teaching may be equitably judged. Enter now the supervisors, bearing notebooks and assurances that they are only there "to help." Despite these assurances, teachers know that whatever happens in class can never be revised. However brilliant the performance yesterday or tomorrow, chances are that the supervisor will remember only what happened today. They know, too, that supervisors who find no cause for improvement in what they observe are likely to find little justification for what they do, and consequently that they are inclined to be more critical than sympathetic about the problems that teaching invariably incurs. And finally they know that although teaching for them is an elusive art, at once personal and subjective, for supervisors it becomes a science about which one may be neutral and objective.

So far as merit is concerned, the notion of accountability is severally flawed. For one thing, to insist that teachers be held accountable is to belabor the obvious. One cannot possibly confront crowds of upturned faces day after day and remain impervious to the responsibility that this entails. Nor can one find an audience that is more outspoken or disdainful in the face of incompetence or neglect than they. Like all performers—be they athletes, musicians, or craftsmen—teachers know more about the quality of their performance than do their spectators. And where they misjudge this quality, as on occasion they are wont to do, their students leave them little room for doubt. To teach is to have at one's disposal each day scores of miniature accountants who assiduously tabulate every move. Witness how long afterwards, and with what devastating accuracy, students not only recall their teachers but mimic them, much to the delight of their peers with whom they have shared the experience. Here is accountability that needs no reminding, amid merit that each hour takes the measure of one's being.

A more serous flaw lies in the assumption that classes may be treated as isolated events, hermetically sealed from outside influence, and consequently reducible to observable behaviors whose causes may be found in the class and the way in which it is conducted on any given day. It is as if classrooms were test tubes from which all pesky variables could be conveniently eliminated. Should the contents of the class be found wanting, then all we need do is change the mix of ingredients—a dash more of this, a spoonful less of that. The job of the supervisor is therefore to analyze the mix and prescribe the necessary alterations. Here the presumption seems to be that learning boasts a smooth trajectory of incremental triumphs that can be programmed at will into some privileged sequence, a sequence that is not only known, but is also capable of being demonstrated beyond dispute. Were this in fact the case, then teachers would no longer need to produce activities for the supervisor to observe, since nothing of value cold be learned either from watching or from teaching.

Still another flaw lies in the implication that only teachers need to be held accountable, not schools. Since teachers are the principal, if not sole, performers, schools assume the guise of employment agencies hired to police migrant personnel. Those who do not pass inspection must go; whereas, the school survives untainted, its standards maintained and its reputation the more enhanced because it has demonstrated the good sense to get rid of "bad teachers." But if teachers are to be held accountable for what happens or does not happen in their classes, for what is the school being held accountable? Come to think of it, what else is there to be accounted for besides instruction? And wherein does the authority or the integrity of the school lie? Hiring teachers? Dispersing community funds? Unless schools can proclaim a stance in education that exceeds a mere taxonomy of lofty virtues, they are in fact little more than employment agencies with no real authority to pass judgment on the quality of teaching. Conversely, if they do articulate such a stance, then they must bear the burden of responsibility for helping their teachers attain the virtues espoused. Were schools thus held accountable, the failure of a teacher would also be considered the failure of the school to educate that teacher, just as now the success of a teacher is deemed a credit to the school.

To speak of merit is to speak of the system of values that fosters it. Here the irony of recent reforms comes fully to light, for the fact is that every school in the country already sponsors a system of merit pay and has it s career ladders firmly in place. Unfortunately, this system of merit, and the rungs by which it ascends, does not include teaching. As everybody knows, one cannot be considered successful in the field of education and remain a teacher. To qualify for merit pay and rise on the ladder of public esteem one must become an administrator.

And upon what does administrative merit and its mounting influence depend? That is peculiarly difficult to answer. All that we can say with certainty is that administrative merit seems to have little or nothing to do with instructional merit. In fact, it is quite possible, and by no means rare, for an individual to rise in the ranks of educational administration without ever having taught. As a rule, however, we find that top administrators do have some teaching experience, if only a few years worth. But instead of paying them a visit to assess their performance, we interview them. In the course of this interview we ask them to explain how they would handle all sorts of hypothetical problems that typically plague schools. If we like what they say, then we hire them at a salary "commensurate with their position." Naturally, the higher the position, the more the administrative experience required. Yet how one acquires administrative experience in the first place or judges it thereafter is never entirely clear.

These considerations aside, we can see clearly enough why merit pay and career ladders for teachers are so controversial. It is not that teaching lacks merit, or even that such merit is too difficult to measure (why not just interview potentially meritorious teachers?). No, the problem is that there is already another hierarchy of merit in place, which because it lacks relevance to teaching cannot be joined. Why initiate a second hierarchy whose topmost rungs reach no higher than the nethermost rungs of the first?

The sad truth is that merit in education is no different from merit anywhere else. What the public values is not education *per se*, but the money and power it yields. What other conclusion is possible about a system that entrusts its minds but not its money to the teacher's care? It is here that we find the distinguishing criterion between teaching and administration, for the one thing that teachers are never allowed to do in a school is decide how its funds shall be spent. Whatever they need they must ask for by seeking approval of an administrator, whether the item in question is a pencil or a computer. What merit can lie in a system that, in effect, requires its practitioners to beg for their tools? One might as well ask doctors to beg for bandages, lawyers for legal research, priests for bread and wine. It is this begging that keeps our drudges humble, for they are granted no voice in deciding what projects shall be funded, what books shall be bought, what equipment shall be ordered, which teachers shall be hired.

What we see in the glass is mirrored in the times—the New York Times and the Los Angeles Times. Under "Careers in Education" we find the image of merit brought into sudden relief, for the pages are filled with enticements for supervisors, principals, superintendents, heads of departments. They speak in glowing terms of the communities, the credentials, the salaries, the requisites for leadership and experience. Down at the bottom of the second page are the listings for teachers, economically phrased as "Openings for math, science, and English." There are no calls for remarkable teachers, no lures of salary, no criteria for sparkling performance or ancillary accomplishments. The message is clear: although careers in education commence with teaching, they do not culminate there.

If teaching is to take place among the higher employments of life, teachers must be attracted by the prospect of good rather than driven by the fear of evil; they must entertain some hope of praise amid the likelihood of censure; and they must anticipate a time when their success can be met with applause and their diligence with reward. But above all, they should be given some sense of equity in their labors, so that as they remove rubbish and clear obstructions from the paths of Learning and Genius, they may share in the conquest and glory that stem from their constant endeavors.

Teacher Souls for Sale

A score of years ago the sister of an erstwhile student of mine accosted me in the hall bearing special news. Her older sister, then in college, had evidently found the answer to nearly everything and wanted me to know.

"Wants me to know the answer," I asked, "or just that she has found it?"

"Both," she said.

"Okay, then, let's have it. What's the answer?"

"Politics," she said, and, relishing my astonishment, swung gleefully down the hall to her next class.

Were this exchange to recur today, my guess is that "politics" would have given way to "economics" as the operative paradigm. These days we want to skip the details of process, our interest lying mainly in "The Bottom Line." The product rather than the process currently preoccupies us, the business of economics having quite thoroughly pervaded our thinking about nearly everything, including, I regret to say, education.

In schools the age of "accountability" is upon us, its cries for "raising the bar" echoing down the legislative corridors throughout the country. And because accountability relies exclusively on that which may be counted, we are inundated with hastily assembled, state mandated tests that at some impending deadline must be passed to gain promotion and ultimately to graduate.

So fortified, education will purportedly rise to meet standards of competence and performance heretofore undreamt of in our philosophy, thus equipping us to meet the harsh demands that the twenty-first century has in store. Schooling will at last become a business in which the quality of the product rides upon the level of competition among rival institutions. Those that do not measure up must face the consequences of their failure, in all probability losing their accreditation, perhaps falling into receivership, whatever this may entail.

Under such dire threats schools quite naturally must accede to teaching, or trying to teach, those facts, concepts, and competencies that are likely to appear on these statewide tests. For better or worse, teachers will teach to the test rather than have their students denied promotion or entry into higher education. What is *worth* knowing and doing will ostensibly fall upon some privileged coterie of sages to decide, highly selective blue ribbon panels that instinctively know what is best for us and for our country. The rest of us must act accordingly, faithfully adhering to the guidelines handed down and dutifully transmitting the wisdom of our superiors, even though the bottom lines thus drawn give us no clue about *how* this wisdom is to be attained.

So much for process. To draw a line is one thing; to reach that line quite another. Even so, we already know that the products incurred are bound to reveal no surprises, given that schools are already in competition. Those with the most money, the newest facilities, and the best educated clientele are clearly slated to score the highest on whatever tests may be administered. Who, then, do we judge accountable for the inner city schools? What students or, for that matter, what teachers will opt to attend and work in these schools? And exactly how are these schools supposed to compete when they have not the wherewithal to do so?

But the trouble does not end here. Recent news from Colorado gives us further cause to doubt the putative advance of educational reform as teachers in Denver agree to a program that ties their pay raises to student performance. Burdened as we already are by the spate of standardized tests now increasingly imposed on students, these latest proposals carry cries for "accountability" beyond the pale. To hold schools solely accountable for the success or failure of their students is to grant teachers more power over their charges than they either have or want. By the same token, for any single measure of achievement to determine the advance or retreat of a child's career is to grant more authority than any test should be allowed to exercise over any taker.

Withal, this latest proposal, just approved by the Denver public schools and supported by that city's teachers' union, gives an ominous twist to our economic paradigm. Designated "Procomp," which suggests a system "for competence" as opposed to incompetence, current staff may choose to join, whereas all new staff must join. What 30% of existing have decided to join is a system of pay that is geared to performance that is variously calculated, depending on test scores and specific schoolwide goals set by the administration and the district. Beyond good teaching, Procomp takes into consideration those positions that have special value; e.g., teaching in tough schools, teaching math or science, special needs, and the like. Be that as it may, let us not get swept up in the particulars of assessment and how it shall be judged. The point is this: teachers will be teaching not for their students, their communities, their ideals; they will now be teaching for themselves, for money. I don't mean that they are not already earning their livelihood and expect to be remunerated for their services. I mean that their interest in learning and teaching will be construed as basically entrepreneurial. They will be singing for their supper, dancing to the mercenary beat.

Consider the impact that this latest move may exert on the spirit as well as the conduct of school. If teachers are essentially to be remunerated on the basis of their students' achievement, or as determined by the administration, which of them will likely opt to teach in our urban settings where education is in greatest disarray? Moreover, which of them will agree to undertake the teaching of chronic underachievers? Will not the most talented classes—the honors and AP's—become the exclusive purview of the veteran teachers? This will leave the most difficult job of teaching in the hands of those least experienced and at the bottom of the pay scale, thus ensuring the least effective instruction, however enthusiastic, for those in greatest need. It will also discourage young teachers from remaining in the classroom, to say nothing of those contemplating entry into the profession.

How will students and parents come to view the efforts of such teachers? Of course the teachers will profess to have their students' intellectual and emotional development at heart, but who will believe them? They'll be like politicians, elected officials whose every action is interpreted as essentially self-serving, calculated to fill their campaign coffers and get them re-elected. Teachers will teach to the test and/or to what their principals favor, whatever this may be and however valid, because their careers will be measured accordingly. Education will thus become a business where the bottom line shall become the only line worth pursuing.

But what is this line that purports to lie at the bottom? The bottom of what? Learning has no bottom, nor for that matter any top. In calling for a bottom line by which the top must also be measured, notice that nothing need be known or learned on the part of the callers—no preparations advised, no strategies offered, no procedures submitted, no solutions proposed, no methodologies, no techniques—nothing save threats and demands. Schools that must bribe their teachers in order to teach their students are schools that know neither how to teach nor how to learn.

We still have yet to plumb the depths of this proposal, however, since it touches upon the very soul of teaching, the soul that lies in the delicate relationship that must preside between teacher and student if learning is to prosper. At the core of this relationship resides the matter of trust. Students must believe that their teachers hold their best interests at heart, will do everything in their power to help them learn, treat their charges fairly, not play favorites, entertain high expectations coupled with realistic demands. Conversely, teachers must believe that their students want to learn, that they will earnestly try to do their teachers' bidding, granting the same respect to them as to the knowledge they wish to acquire.

Consider not only the time that students and teachers spend together, but also the very special quality that this time must preserve. Hour upon hour, day upon day, week after week they meet to pursue their mutual topics. Teachers and students talk about things they share with no one else, nowhere else—not with friends, not with family. They consider ideas and concepts that may have no direct bearing on the marketplace but that last a lifetime. And even though students may forget the actual substance of these manifold conversations, they vividly remember every one of their teachers and the relationship that they bore with each.

Inject into this unique relationship the matter of money. As a student I now know that, particulars notwithstanding, my relationship with my teacher is no longer unique, no longer special. It is a relationship similar to that between customer and entrepreneur. Now, instead of knowing and liking me, my teacher wants me to learn in order to make a profit from our efforts. Knowledge is not to be had because it is worth knowing but because it is worth money, at least for the teachers. Teaching has therefore become like selling cars or insurance: the more you sell the more you earn.

Why should teaching be treated differently from other professions? Do we pay doctors according to how many diseases they cure? Perhaps we should institute a body count: those with the fewest dead bodies get paid the most for their "competency," irrespective of the diseases their patients may incur. What about lawyers? Shall we pay them according to the number of convictions they win or by how many criminals they successfully defend?

When commercial interests finally penetrate the halls of academe and schools become "data driven," teaching shall be laid open to avarice. How much is great teaching worth? How can such teaching be repaid? It can't be; it is a gift, which largely defines its greatness. Will my students love and honor me because I am rich? Dishonor me because I am poor? What about the students who fail? Shall I practice triage and decide to concentrate on those students who prove most profitable? Will a certain segment of society be deemed a bad educational investment and thereby ignored? And how much might I charge a girl who learns the answer for nearly everything?

Teaching is an investment of the heart, not of the pocketbook. Make of it a business and we steal its soul.

Tinker's Rule:

Crafting Careers for Teachers[10]

When I applied for my first teaching job, the interviewer—a Mr. Tinker by name—told me that it took five years to make an English teacher. At the time I thought this extravagant, ostensibly the boast of an elder anxious to magnify his labors. With a master's degree in hand, the arrogance of youth at heart, and a whole semester of student teaching under my belt, surely I could be exempted from Tinker's rule. After all, one need only codify one's accumulated notes, peruse the assigned texts, and get a decent night's sleep to ensure the obedience, awe, and devotion of one's prospective students. The rest would come to me as the need arose.

But forty-five years of teaching have convinced me that Tinker was right, indeed, profoundly optimistic in his assessment. I have been reminded of his rule in reading about the current controversy over teacher preparation and testing. I have no quarrel with tightening the standards maintained by our higher institutions of learning, to say nothing of our lower institutions of learning where I continue to labor, "doomed," as Dr. Samuel Johnson once characterized himself, "only to remove rubbish and clear obstructions from the paths of Learning and Genius, who press forward to conquest and glory without bestowing a smile on the humble drudge that facilitates their progress." Be they ever so humble, is it too much to ask that our teachers become literate and more than modestly informed, not only about their chosen fields of study, but also about the world at large? Clearly not. But let us not dismiss the problem as one of standards alone, no matter how much such standards may be in need of repair, whether in schools, colleges, or graduate schools of education.

No, the difficulty runs deeper than this. What we have here is a structural problem inherent in the way we traditionally think about teaching.

Take the present controversy about testing teachers. Of course we want all our teachers to be able to pass the test, leaving aside the issues of exactly what and how such tests may be testing. But supposing every teacher did pass—what then? Would our problems thereby be solved? Probably not, for to understand the implications of Tinker's rule is to accede to the realization that knowledge alone is not enough. Teachers can be told all manner of things about teaching and their subject matter, touching upon curriculum, clever strategies, aims and objectives, modes of assessment, cooperative learning, what have you. In any day's worth of junk mail delivered to our schools, we find all the putative guarantees and solutions we could want for ensuring success in education. But in the real world—and contrary to popular opinion, schools constitute a world as real as any other—to learn how to teach one has to teach. There is no substitute for it, no certification of it officially or otherwise, for teaching is itself a form of learning that cannot be taught, an art that must be exhaustively practiced before it can be mastered. And even then its success is by no means assured.

That is the thrust of Tinker's rule, though not the full length and breadth of its implications. As every parent knows, a school is only as good as its teachers. And as every teacher knows, a class can only be as good as its students. It is this interaction between teacher and student that is the crux of education—what each brings to the table, then takes away from that table. In his famous essay on "What is a University?" Cardinal Newman maintained that "the general principles of any study you may learn by books at home, but the detail, the color, the tone, the air, the life which makes it live in us, you must catch all these from those in whom it lives already." Knowledge lives in teachers who are kept alive with the prospect of advancing their own expertise as well as that of their students. To expect that some battery of tests, whether imposed upon teachers, students, or both, will significantly alter that critical interaction in the classroom is simply to rehearse an ancient mistake in the annals of education.

Just as parents cannot expect schools to overcome years of neglect in their children, neither should legislators expect teachers to learn the art of teaching merely from tests or texts, nor from schools of education. And those who prate about holding teachers suddenly "accountable" have either never known or too soon forgotten the accountability that lives in the eyes of every student who sits and watches teachers hour after hour all the livelong day. We can no longer afford to throw teachers at students and expect either to flourish. It is high time we held schools and the communities that support them accountable for educating and training their teachers, not for five years or ten, but for as long as they continue to teach children.

Why is it that institutions devoted to learning are so recalcitrant in educating themselves? In public schools, after teachers receive favorable assessments from an administrator for the initial three years of employment, they are often granted tenure for the rest of their careers, irrespective of what else they may learn or do by way of instruction. They are paid according to the number of degrees they garner from outside and the number of years they survive. Short of molesting a child or succumbing to drug abuse, their jobs are secure. They are represented by strong unions that negotiate their wages and working conditions. Meanwhile, they earn "PDP's" (professional development points) for attending occasional workshops on a variety of topics that may or may not impinge on their subject areas. Other than advanced degrees obtained on their own time and at their own expense, the only promotion available to them besides longevity is administration. The best that teachers can hope for is to be removed from the classroom.

What kind of profession is this where the best practitioners are rewarded for ceasing to practice? And why do we believe that testing new teachers and getting rid of bad teachers will significantly improve education? The fallacy is precisely that of the excluded middle, of overlooking what teachers might conceivably learn between initiation and termination, even when their careers may stretch over half a century. Surely there is more to say about teaching than its hiring and firing. The question is what they need to know, what they need to learn, what they need to do, and what prevents them from knowing, learning, and doing whatever they should. To expect teachers to excel is to grant them the luxury of having a career, to give them the benefit of earning the status of a true profession.

What does it mean to treat teaching as a career? We can begin by asking what might constitute an ideal career in teaching, what changes it incurs, what goals it should pursue, what experiences it can include, what milestones it must negotiate, and in general how its culmination may differ from its commencement. So viewed, we can begin to envision a great deal that one must learn about schooling in general and about teaching in particular over the course of a single career. In the first five years of teaching, for example, teaching assignments need to be carefully orchestrated to ensure that individuals are not inundated with too many students and too many preparations. They need to be linked closely with a mentor who can offer constructive criticism and modeling, who can teach beside them. They need to observe others teach. They should be trained in the use of all the technology available in the school. They need to explore the full range of offerings and be exposed to all levels of student achievement and abilities.

With increasing experience teachers need to branch out, supervising an extracurricular activity, coaching a sport so as to ensure alternative venues in which to interact with students. Every teacher should be presumed to possess certain talents and strengths that need to be augmented and utilized. They should be encouraged to develop a specialty in addition to contributing to the established curriculum. At some point they should be encouraged and financially supported to undertake graduate studies. It should be assumed that, like everyone else, teachers need special considerations at different times in their lives: for families, for injuries, illnesses, financial obligations. Ultimately, they need to take part in every aspect of schooling, be it coaching, extracurricular activities, administration, curriculum, publishing, professional involvement, supervision, research, finance, special needs, teacher training.

Albeit unique, teaching is not unlike most other vocations in certain respects. If you work in a bank, you have to learn banking. If you want to start a restaurant, you have to know more than cooking. If you join the military, you have to learn how to conduct a war. Why is it not obvious that teachers' careers need to be planned from start to finish, not by administrators, consultants, school boards, or legislators, nor yet by specially appointed "blue ribbon" panels, but by teachers themselves who need to define and stipulate the ground rules and milestones of their profession and in so doing make it truly their own? Every teacher should be following a career path especially designed with and for them. They should be paid in accordance with their progress in completing each step along that path, however long it lasts.

At one of the retirement parties occurring at the end of every school year, I remember in particular a teacher who had managed to teach and to retain her dignity over nearly half a century. She was one who would have had no difficulty passing a teacher's test. And in the little speech she gave at the end of her career she talked about the number of times she had mounted the steps to her classroom on the fourth floor. It was considered her classroom because it was the very same one she occupied in her first year at the school and in every year thereafter for almost half a century. She ended up doing exactly what she had started doing in that first year: she had a homeroom, classes of English, lunch duty, study halls, supervision of assigned extracurricular activities. The number of cumulative steps she had assiduously counted going up and down those stairs was truly staggering, positively Sisyphean. Everyone was very impressed, we toasted her, and she left.

I am saddened to think that so fine and upstanding a teacher as this should have had no more to say or to show about her career than the number of steps she ascended on her way to class. However much she may have contributed to children, and I have no cause to doubt that she did, she left without telling us anything about what happened once she got to class. One can only imagine what such a devoted servant might have achieved had she been encouraged to convey her triumphs as well as her tribulations, her tests and techniques, her revelations and insights, the breadth and depth of her learning, her ambitions and accomplishments. She was allowed not to have any of these, at least none that others could discern and apply to their own endeavors. Perhaps for the administration she was an ideal teacher, always tidy and on time, keeping things calm, reliable at lunch duty, a stickler for attendance. But for the rest of us she might just as well have been a ghost.

Our schools are filled with ghosts who labor quietly behind closed doors, humble drudges from whom we have neither the wit nor the wherewithal to demand a full and enterprising career, whether it comprises five years or fifty.

Making the Difference[11]

On the road to Greensboro, fresh from breakfast at the K & W Cafeteria—orange juice, grits, waffles, bacon, and all the coffee you can drink, all for $3.85—we are in high spirits. We call ourselves "The B Team," a six-man strike force plying the interior of North Carolina in a rented van, searching for minority teacher candidates willing to brave the icy winters of Greater Boston.

At the wheel is Sam Turner, principal of the Ward School in Newton. Next to him, dwarfing the bucket seat, Al Fortune, principal of the Pierce School in Brookline. In the middle seats, Dick Sederstrom and I: Sederstrom, Director of Personnel for the Concord Public Schools; myself, chairman of the English department at Brookline High School. In back, Ed Fraktman and Jim Marini, principals in Newton and Concord respectively, engage in a permanent discussion about teachers and schools, parents and kids. Together we represent the Personnel Administrators' Collaborative (PAC), a consortium of fourteen school systems in Greater Boston who join forces in an effort to bring qualified minority teachers to the area.

Map in hand, Sederstrom directs us through the bypasses and down the freeways as we thread our way west from Durham to Winston-Salem and back again to Greensboro. Tireless and canny in the complexities of finding and hiring teachers from across the country, he is a frequent traveler and our navigator. As signs for Greensboro flash by overhead, he hurries to identify the proper exit, but this time Sam knows the way. He has been visiting schools down here for the past eighteen years, luring his people north. Turners seem to reside in every town we enter, including Greensboro.

Swinging off the freeway on the outskirts of town, we notice that it doesn't look as prosperous as Durham or Winston-Salem, where we have been recruiting for the past two days. Many of the houses are of the 1920's bungalow variety with low-slung shingled porches across the front, solid metal porch furniture painted green, and pinched dormer windows winking from their slanted roofs. The rest are of ever-popular southern brick, small but neat, also with porches and aluminum filigree.

In the center of town Al Fortune points out the now famous Woolworth's, whose lunch counter figured so centrally in the civil rights movement. Commanding in bulk, avuncular in manner, Al is a charter member of PAC and a familiar figure in these parts, although a native New Englander. Early last September, upon seeing an unbroken circle of white faces at Brookline's orientation session for new teachers, I had asked Al, "What ever happened to affirmative action?" His answer was a plane ticket to North Carolina.

On the next rise we see the cluster of buildings that is our destination: North Carolina A & T University. Yesterday we stopped off to see Chapel Hill, the first university in the state. There bell towers tolled hymns, domed and pillared edifices ornamented quadrangles and stately tree-lined walks. We visited the campus's new temple for basketball, seating some 23,000. Next to this massive, bunker-like structure stretched a separate building for aquatics, long as an airplane hanger, with two pools laid end to end.

Greensboro's A & T State University is no match for Chapel Hill. Rectangular brick buildings, some of them new, seem randomly placed, their hard edges unbroken by trees or shrubs, their small windows unadorned. No pillars or domes, no stately quads nor bell towers grace this once separate but unequal institution where our own Jim Cradle earned his degree. This will be our last stop.

In the parking lot we see the now familiar faces of our fellow recruiters who have accompanied us these past two days. Teams from California, Denver, Seattle, South Bend, Shaker Heights, Atlanta, Miami, Cincinnati, Rochester, Lansing, Portland (Oregon), Tampa, and Tallahassee all converge to draw from this watershed of teacher education. But the bulk of recruiters represent school systems from the middle Atlantic states—Maryland, Virginia, North and South Carolina. Dade County needs to hire 500 new teachers; so does Cincinnati.

Most teams bring only literature, some display banners—Indian River and Rochester—and a few bring portable booths replete with spotlights and pictures. Caroline Blue from Prince George's County, Maryland—a large black woman strikingly dressed—offers new teachers an incentive program: one month's free rent, discounts on loans, Visa and Mastercards, restaurants, and dealer cost on new Fords.

Nancy Driscoll and Marcella Thomas from Raleigh have formed their own consulting service (Educational Personnel Development Systems) to supply school systems with minority candidates. They have modeled their strategies on what they have learned from watching Al Fortune and Sam Turner.

As before, we will be situated in the gym, this one also new and designed mainly for basketball. Inside we find the playing floor centrally placed a couple of stories below the ground level, from which grandstands cascade on all sides to the brightly painted floor. At the ground level the grandstands have been folded back into each of the four surrounding walls, exposing a mezzanine floor about as wide as a three-lane highway. In this space, 163 tables have been set up with tablecloths and signs to accommodate school systems who will comprise today's Teacher Fair.

Concord and Brookline have been assigned to booths at opposite ends of the gym. Fortune is worried. With our team divided, it will be difficult to work the floor and the doors. Our tactic is to have four at the tables and two scouting the floor, rounding up abashed and errant candidates. Yesterday at Winston-Salem we interviewed forty-five candidates while other recruiters sat waiting at their tables and talked to three. We decide that, during the opening ceremonies and the lunch that will follow, we will move Concord and Brookline and appropriate some extra chairs.

An air of formality and excitement pervades all of these functions. The facilities are spotless, the food generous, and the schedule supremely organized. Recruiters are provided with special lounges, coffee and donuts. They are greeted by the presiding officials of the university and introduced to representatives from all the schools who will be supplying candidates. We hear about excellence in education, the need for high standards, and scores on the National Teacher Exam. The speakers call for cooperation and wish us success in placement. Organizers of the fair are cheerful and cordial, anxious to please. This is their bread and butter, for here teaching is perceived as a respected profession, an instrument of upward mobility, an industry for human potential.

Each of the institutions we have visited was once a black teachers' college, similar to our old normal schools. One of the few professions open to the blacks, teaching has always flourished here. Despite poor facilities and meager funds, these institutions persevered through the fifties and sixties and expanded and consolidated through the seventies and eighties as state funds were slowly pried loose. Here, Maynard Jackson, first black mayor of Atlanta, got his start along with Earl "The Pearl" Monroe, Jesse Jackson, Clarence "Jeep" Jones, and Ron McNair, to say nothing of the hundreds and thousands who have recently entered the teaching field.

To these fairs come the neighboring schools—Shaw University, Spellman, St. Augustine, Wake Forest, Hampton, High Point, Fiske, and Bennett College—the black Wellesley of the South. At BU, BC, Northeastern, Tufts, Wellesley, Harvard, Simmons, and Wheelock, only a handful of minority students resort to teaching. That is why we are here.

Sederstrom, Marini, Fortune, and Turner head for Woolworth's to enjoy a historical lunch. Fraktman and I decide to stay, on the chance we can catch a few early birds who wander in unawares. By the time our teammates return, we already have two at the table. With the rumble of feet and the din of voices mounting to a thunderous pitch, we are off and running.

No sooner do we finish with the first pair than Sam delivers half a dozen Bennett girls who look bemused but stunned by his disarming cackle, at once evil and jovial. As we double up the girls, interviewing two at a time, Fortune heads for the doors. First we have them fill out the cards— name, address, telephone, target grade level, special interest. Across from us Rochester and Indian River sit alone, reading their books, but covertly watching all the commotion.

Our object is to make a fast assessment and then hardsell teaching in the cradle of liberty. We are looking for the "heavy hitters," the "blue chippers," whom we pass around to check out our perceptions and to take up their time. We score them "1+" and grade the rest down to "3." From the 150 candidates we will eventually interview in the course of three days, 20 will be invited on an expense-free trip to Boston where they will be put up by local families, tour Boston (Quincy Market, Filene's

Basement), and interview at a couple of member school systems, each of whom has contributed $1000 for this collaborative service. Since a single advertisement in the Boston Globe costs $600, PAC dues are a bargain. Of the twenty students invited, perhaps three or four will ultimately be hired by the fourteen participating schools systems.

However small the yield, we are too busy to think about that now. Turner and Fortune are delivering a steady stream and our throats are getting dry. Sederstrom and Marini are at one table, Fraktman and I at the other. This youthful parade produces individuals who are collectively inspiring. Immaculately dressed, they wear three-piece suits, tailored dresses. Ties and handkerchiefs are conservative and color coordinated; jewelry, muted and tasteful; shoes, shined. There are no sweatshirts or jeans, no sneakers. Each carries a briefcase from which is proudly extracted a perfect resume, all formatted exactly the same, depending on the institution attended. Their answers are fluent and rehearsed.

We want them all, but in the press of time must concentrate on those who clearly stand out. Few have been north of Washington, D.C. We speak as if from a foreign country—arctic in climate, staid in isolate traditions. We find the Bennett girls stiff and proper, compulsively attentive and polite. Fortune and Turner help to loosen them up, but not much. They are surprised and a little suspicious to learn that we do not require scores on the National Teacher Examination. They are still more astonished to hear that we do not rely heavily on commercial texts. We explain that despite the lack of exams and dearth of texts, our expectations are high. We believe that education rests in the hands of teachers, and that by hiring the best teachers we can find we vouchsafe our students' learning. They are pleased with this answer and visibly brighten.

The standouts make our day. They are fresh and natural, lively and attractive. David Chambers is mine. Taking a break, I find him standing at the main entrance, surveying the sea of tables and not knowing where to start, which is precisely how I would feel. I introduce myself and invite him to join us. He looks relieved. Handsome and shy, but graced with a big smile, he is a social studies major and a wide receiver, wants to teach high school. Ramona D. Gerald is from Lumberton, North Carolina, interested in elementary K-4. She is described as "a Sam Turner special . . . a super young lady, poised, well-groomed, articulate, talented." She will get invited. Clay Terrel was raised on a farm with five siblings, works a forty-hour week to support himself at college, wants to teach health and physical education. Jean Elizabeth McCall is poised and articulate, has a strong music background, and wants to teach elementary school.

At a quarter to five we are still busy while most of the other recruiters are packing up for the trip home. We have interviewed fifty candidates, and I am typing up the cards on my portable laptop computer. A couple of teams stop by to ask me what I am doing. Educational Personnel Development Systems is interested in this new wrinkle. I wave my 3 1/2 inch disk and tell them we will offer them a copy of our list for a nominal consulting fee. They say they have a computer at home. We say we will have the letters out by tomorrow. Next year, we predict, they will have their own portable laptop computer.

At the airport lounge in Greensboro, waiting for our flight home, Fraktman and Marini are still talking about teachers and schools, parents and kids. But on one point they now agree: we are the "A Team," not the "B." Sederstrom is rubbing his hands in anticipation of hosting the heavy hitters in April. Turner is staying over to visit his sister and return the van to Durham.

Fortune leans over to show me a note he received from one of his teachers. Beginning her kindergarten at Pierce School this year, a tiny black girl told her parents at dinner, "Hey, I just noticed my whole school is black. Well, the person who's in charge of everybody is black."

"What do you think about that?" asked the parents.

"Well, I think it's good. Then people that are black will appreciate their color."

Nothing Gold Can Stay[12]

O ur perennial demise is once again at hand. We sense it first in the light that begins to linger as the days wax longer, now illuminating our journeys home, then pressing on towards dinner. But yesterday, it seems, we drove and dined in darkness, only to arise the next morning and find our windows still black. Now we notice the grass no longer frosted beige but flecked with green; the worn paths hardened with winter's sheen have turned soft and dark, giving off the scent that we had forgotten earth possessed. One day soon the peepers will greet the twilight, then the forsythia will break, daffodils dot the yard out back, and stark trees push forth their gilded canopies.

It is this time of year when instruction weighs heaviest on our souls, our heads bleary with distinctions that have long since lost their edge, our hearts weary with broken promises and threadbare excuses from our students who slog through their lessons as if learning were a calculated affront.

In these sodden days we look back to crisp September with chagrin, when everything had again seemed possible, and when we relinquished our summer's ease with a mounting sense of excitement. As our leaders ritually assured us, this would be the year in which all systems would flawlessly perform, this the year when no student would fall through the cracks and every mind would open to everything we had in store. It would be a year in which our valued contributions would at last attain the recognition they so richly deserved, and when together we would find cause to celebrate the conquest of ignorance. Or something like that. And so we marched off happily to class to greet our new charges, still featureless as they sat quietly arrayed before us while we mispronounced their names.

Those first days are golden. Autumn to the world, they are education's spring. Still rested and glowing, we are secretly glad to be back, ready to take up our calling once again. Summer stories fill coffee and lunch as we negotiate our transition. We labor to imbue our prior days of licensed ease with levity and significance that they cannot retain much longer. Still, new books smell just the same as they always did when we were in school and stuck our noses between the pages to sniff the print. And the redolence of freshly sharpened pencils reassures us that all is well. We accept our stiff new grade books, their pages crisply lined but as yet unthumbed and bearing no traces of triumph, mediocrity, or failure. Bereft of names and unmarred by agonizing decision, they signify the awesome trust granted to us by people we know nothing of, confirming that we shall be given another chance to prove our worth.

All this is but a prelude to the first class, when after the hopes and promises have been duly delivered authority reverts to the teachers. It is a beginning we must create with pomp and circumstance. Walking into that first class, we momentarily busy ourselves, writing our name and course title on the board, fidgeting with the computer printout of the class list to give our students a chance to glean their first impressions. We know it is the first day because all the sneakers gleam shiny white from underneath the desks, having been removed from their boxes only the day before. As we read down the list of names we realize that this particular gathering of students seems to be totally indistinguishable one from another, giving us cause to wonder how their individuality will ever emerge. And yet, as we glimpse their attentive faces, the weight of our responsibility comes into sudden focus. Those of us who have our own children know how far these have come, how great an investment each one represents. I have them fill out cards to give me a chance to examine them and establish initial contact in the process of retrieving these forms. I am interested in their penmanship, their questions, and whether their parents' names are singular or different from their own.

And now the speech that I have been tacitly rehearsing ever since receiving the principal's letter in the waning days of August, reminding me that I am employed. My task is to find exactly the right tone, to appear serious enough to jolt them from their summer ennui and make them feel they are back in school. But sincerity must be laced with informality and understated humor to reassure them that the seeming distance between us can be bridged. I tell them that first days are best because there is no work to do and because they still promise infinite possibilities. So far as I know, they are the best students I have ever had, just as I may still be the best teacher they have ever had. Each of us starts cleanly. With time, of course, our reputations will undergo revision as we get to know each other. But for now we must grant each other the highest esteem because our relationship is permanent: I will always be their teacher and they will always be my students. This relationship is one of trust and mutual obligation. I am obliged to teach them what I know, and they are obligated to learn all they can. As relationships go, that between teacher and student is unique. We do not know each other and yet we are bound by this sacred trust. As my students, they have first call upon my time for whatever reason. As their teacher, I have the right to demand from them their best performance. If for any reason we give each other cause to question this trust, then it is broken and nothing further stands to be learned, for learning itself is a kind of trust requiring absolute honesty. This is all they need to know.

In truth, it is a sobering and rather dour little speech, for me as well as for them, but afterwards I never have to refer to rules or punishments. The fact is that youth both understands and values matters of trust. I would hazard the opinion that on the whole they are the most loyal and trustworthy creatures on earth and as such eminently teachable. Like us, however, they are troubled and weak. Whoever has cause to envy youth has lived long enough to forget what it is like. Irremediably social, they are enslaved by their need for attention. Haplessly swung by moods, they ride the full range of emotion. Wanting most to be adults, they are unable to fathom the temperance that only proper seasoning can avail. Anger and hate, love and devotion they comprehend, but restraint and perfection they abhor.

And so it is with the coming of spring that we begin to lose them. Creatures of the sun, their minds progressively melt with warmth as they rediscover their bodies so safely hidden under winter's wraps. Before the splendor of reawakening nature, our carefully wrought lessons and elegant concepts start to crumble. It is then that we recall the ultimate difficulty of our task and steel ourselves against its gradual dismemberment. In desperation we pile on the work to effect a strong finish, unaware that we, too, are in the grip of nature and can no longer maintain the blazing pace of autumn. As we weaken they gather strength and begin to swagger in the certain knowledge that our mission is drawing to a close.

We must lose them, at least for now. Most of them will be back again in a slightly altered form. The freshmen in particular, who seemed so tiny in September, will lie about their homes and grow like zucchini. Upperclassmen will change more subtly, their features better defined and their manner more carefully smoothed. We will see them in the halls and they will brighten, for now there is a special understanding that only we possess. We have told them all our secrets, shared with them what we tell no other living souls—not our friends or our families. And they have anguished and struggled before us, sharing the best that they can think.

As for the graduates, they will surface sporadically at unpredictable moments, anxious to convey the tenor of their new experience, yet wanting to be remembered as only we can remember them. They will see us as having somehow been arrested in our journey, while they have proudly sprinted forth to bigger and better places. Proud of their advance, they are nonetheless nostalgic for the place they knew so well, the place to which they can in fact never return. We will see them less and less, eventually forgetting their names but not their quirks, until all but a few will disappear altogether.

Teaching is one of the very few vocations that is annually destroyed. In summer we are stripped of our calling, bereft of the relationships so assiduously nurtured throughout the year. Our gradebooks, meticulously maintained and well thumbed are suddenly irrelevant. We are like tourists in our own hometowns where people we do not know find no special cause for admiration or trust. Scattered abroad upon the face of the earth, we await another rebirth.

THE SCHOOL

A Philosophy for High School

A philosophy is not a curriculum, not a showcase in which all the education wares of a school, be they conventional or unique, are placed on display for public inspection and approval. School philosophies should rather be vehicles for introspection whose purpose is to guide, confirm, and incite thought about the ways in which knowledge is imparted and acquired. A philosophy of education should articulate a set of attitudes that underlies the various teaching and learning styles operating in a school, styles that reflect the thinking of those who live there. Accordingly, one might consider the following observations as a basis for such a philosophy.

Education Examines Not the Individual but the Species

The value of learning lies not so much in its immediate utility as in its generality. Schools are instituted and maintained to serve their communities as havens of learning, not as microcosms of the marketplace. Here students are apprenticed to life in its ideal form—life that is devoted to inquiry, touched by beauty, informed by justice, guided by reason, girded by simplicity, graced by elegance. At the very least, graduates should exhibit competency in certain skills—composition, computation—but the aim is to make them literate about the full array of human achievement, so that they will know what it means to do anything well.

No Style of Learning or Teaching is Privileged

Learning and teaching are inseparable. Both rely on a sense of timing, a state of readiness, a heightened sensibility that enables one to see or say or think something not seen or said or thought before. Readiness is achieved in different ways, depending on what there is to be learned. Sometimes it requires painful and protracted effort—thinking, reading, watching, writing, talking, doing. Other times it is attained effortlessly, almost inadvertently. Either way, timing is critical. Knowing how to learn or how to teach is essentially knowing when to press and when to let go. Styles of learning and teaching are characterized by their mix of pressure and patience. Thorough education will expose teachers and students to a range of styles so that they may come to know their own.

Learning is a Mixture of Pleasure and of Pain

The love of learning is an acquired taste, an addiction for the tart rather than the sweet. To learn is to change and to change can be both exhilarating and wrenching. As creatures of habit, we must approach learning with trepidation, not expecting those who learn to experience a smooth trajectory of triumphs, nor those who teach to affect unrelieved excitement for their subject. While it is true that what is most easily learned is usually hardest taught, it is also true that love of learning cannot be taught; it can only be exemplified. As is so often averred, teaching requires patience. Let it also be said that what teaching requires, learning must learn.

Thoughtfulness is the Social as well as the Intellectual Aim of Education.

The habit of reflection is the ideal trait of the educated mind, taking for its concern what others may be satisfied to take for granted. Education should foster this habit, should teach us patience in the construction and understanding of ideas. But it should also teach us to consider feelings, to anticipate the probable effect of our words and actions on others, and to temper these when they augur injury. Education is thus forethought as well as afterthought, abiding thought rather than sporadic thought.

Education Presumes a Climate of Care

The schoolhouse must be a kind of home that offers its inhabitants a sense of belonging, of individuality strengthened by expectation, of security born of respect. As in the home, the student should feel known but revered; the teacher, exposed but esteemed. Reason should prevail and, where reason falls short, tolerance preside. Regard for excellence need not preclude acceptance of human foible; neither should devotion and understanding be devoid of rigor. Care is by nature compensatory, seeking to provide that which would otherwise be lacking.

Greetings from Mr. Gladgrind[13]

I magine for a moment that you are a new teacher at an orientation session held at the beginning of the school year. It is late August. The ground is dry, the leaves dusty, and already the light has begun to shift. The Dean of Faculty rises to address the coterie of new staff gathered in the library.

"Good morning. On behalf of our parents, students, and staff let me welcome you to the Lighthouse Public Schools. My name is Gladgrind. We are impressed with your credentials and hope to improve them. Naturally, your first year here will be a little rocky, but with time we expect that you will enhance your understanding of the subject matter you teach and in so doing will eventually make a significant contribution to education both here and abroad. Of course, you have your working life to achieve that mark. It is not for us to decide the nature of that contribution, but we do hope to shape your career so that you can make the best use of your talents.

"Our first order of business is your schedule. Every effort has been made to meet your expressed inclinations. At the same time, we feel strongly that in your initial years here you should receive as broad an exposure as practicable to the various aspects of your discipline and your school. Each of our schools and departments has invested massive amounts of time to designing what they feel to be the necessary components of a career in teaching. Eventually you will have taught all grades at all levels. As your experience broadens, however, we will also expect you to determine what special course you would like to follow. Time in your career schedule has been set aside for this, as you will observe on the appropriate table in Chapter II of your Handbooks. You will initially be assigned a reduced schedule and shall be allied with an experienced teacher who through broad experience and consistent excellence in teaching shall be designated your personal mentor. Throughout your first year of teaching at Lighthouse we shall be providing you with regular seminars and a retreat designed to orient you to the Lighthouse way of teaching.

"Although your classroom will naturally serve as the prime vehicle of instruction, we here at Lighthouse feel that the beacon of learning should illuminate all corners of a school. In accordance with your interests we will therefore expect you to take part in selected schoolwide activities where interaction with students is likely to be more informal, more varied, and often more intense. Among these activities, we shall eventually wish to appoint you to a part time administrative position so that you may become cognizant of the demands of schoolkeeping and help us to improve the running of the school. Let me emphasize that, perhaps unlike other school systems, we believe administration to be an integral part of teaching and consequently subservient to it. All of our administrators are accomplished teachers who are still engaged in practicing their art.

"If there is any hierarchy at Lighthouse, it occurs in teaching. You will have noticed on your salary schedules, which are inserted at the back of Chapter III of the Handbook, that the traditional slots for master's, master's plus thirty, and doctoral degrees have been omitted. In their place we have substituted the titles "Associate Teacher," "Master Teacher," and "Mentor." These titles represent what is probably best described as plateaus of learning and achievement. Since the general requirements subsumed under these titles are spelled out in detail in your Handbooks, I shall not take time to enumerate them here. Suffice it to say that they have been very carefully worked out by a Task Force headed by our Director of Personnel and consisting of parents, staff, and students. Appointments are made by our Personnel Review Board, which meets annually and enjoys a constituency similar to that of the Task Force. Although appointments are by no means automatic, we feel that we have developed a rigorous but equitable system for judging your progress.

"I should emphasize, however, that these appointments are intended not to encourage favoritism but to create incentive and to reward excellence. In effect, they make explicit what is usually left implicit in school policies, and being implicit is open to the charge of favoritism with regard to promotions. Our aim is not only to develop excellence in teaching in a systematic way, but also to maintain that excellence once it has been developed. To proclaim excellence is one thing; to achieve it, quite another. Recognizing how truly exacting this goal is in time and sustained effort, each successive appointment grants to its recipient more time and greater remuneration to create the excellence that we seek.

"For this notable advance in the professionalism of education we have our community to thank. Faced with declining enrollments, crippling tax restrictions, galloping inflation, and the prospect of losing our best students and teachers to private education, our community has decided to make public education work. They have wisely perceived that the quality of their schools is the most important determinant of the quality of life in their town and that the quality of schools, in turn, depends on the quality of their teaching staff. Our seats of mastery and chairs of mentorship are thus a result of the cooperation among all concerned: individuals, corporations, merchants, parents, residents, students, and teachers alike. Through their contributions in a one-time investment we have managed to endow in perpetuity excellence in education through superb teaching.

"Let me now close with some words of advice and encouragement. Many teachers new to Lighthouse wonder about our mastery and mentor requirements to innovate and eventually to publish. I want to assure those of you who, for one reason or another, are unable or do not choose to meet these exacting requirements, that you will not perish. After all, schools cannot expect to employ only master teachers and mentors. At the same time, providing that the decisions we make together in designing your career are sound and realistic, I am confident that as you progress in your career you will discover some things that, however difficult to express, are nonetheless worthy of sharing in print. In so doing, you will be taking part not just in the lives and education of our students, but in those of students everywhere as well. Surely this is worth striving for.

"Allow me to conclude with some words of wisdom that may help to sustain you in your cause. They are taken from Emerson's famous essay, 'Self Reliance.'

> In every work of genius we recognize our own rejected thoughts;
> they come back to us with a certain alienated majesty. Great works
> of art have no more affecting lesson for us than this. They teach us
> to abide by our spontaneous impression with good-humored
> inflexibility then most when the whole cry of voices is on the other

side. Else tomorrow a stranger will say with masterly good sense precisely what we have thought and felt all the time, and we shall be forced to take with shame our own opinion from another.

"As we say at Lighthouse, 'The lamp of learning is but an inward beam.'"

"Good luck! See you on Monday."

First Day

G ood morning. I am Mr. Rockland, your principal, and happy to see your smiling faces at our first assembly this year.

This morning I would like to share with you a few remarks as we inaugurate your first year at Lighthouse. Your purpose here is to become educated, but what do we mean by that? Acquisition of knowledge is surely a part of this education, yet by no means the whole, for there is another ingredient of greater importance, an ingredient we call wisdom, which is perhaps best defined by that notable scholar Alfred North Whitehead as 'the way in which knowledge is held.'

At Lighthouse we believe thoughtfulness to be the wellspring of this special ingredient called wisdom, which is our quarry. By thoughtfulness we mean not one but several things. To begin with, we want you to be literally full of thought by giving you a great many things to think about. And what you think about must be not only the knowledge you are acquiring, but also the questions that such knowledge implies. If you are learning about the structure of atoms, for example, you need to ask yourselves whether matter can be so neatly divided and classified, whether it is reasonable to assume that all things are formed from one thing or even several things, for this is what the theory of atoms implies. When you are reading great literature you need to consider how it is that truth can emerge from fiction, how what is true can derive from what is essentially a beautiful lie. And when you study mathematics, you need to ponder how symbolic systems, however elegant in their internal consistencies, can possibly account for natural phenomena that appear to be so riven by chance.

Thoughtfulness also means developing the habit of thinking. To be educated is surely to know what others have thought. To be truly educated, however, is to develop a sense of what you yourselves think quite apart from others. You are here to learn from us, yes, but in so doing your final obligation is to learn about yourselves. For the real object of learning is to surpass what is already known, to strike out on your own and ultimately to create knowledge that others may see fit to learn. Such creativity presumes an independence of mind that, although broadly informed, nevertheless comes to rely more and more on its own power and inclination.

Lastly, and perhaps most important, to be thoughtful is to become increasingly mindful of others. Thoughtfulness in this sense is the capacity to displace oneself, to understand how others think and feel, and to see the world from their point of view. To be thoughtful is thus to be considerate of others, to put ourselves in their place, and to do unto them as we would have them do unto us in accordance with the well-known golden rule.

In sum, if wisdom is the way in which knowledge is held, then thoughtfulness is the vessel that holds this knowledge, shapes it, and readies it for use. At Lighthouse the aim of education is to fashion such vessels, and so to prepare you for whatever you are destined to encounter in the world at large. Jesus, one of the world's great teachers, said, "To whom much is given, much is also required." This, then, is what we shall now try to give and what we shall in turn require of you: thoughtfulness that leads to wisdom, creation of a way in which your knowledge may best be held.

May this year be the one that transforms your thought and your life for the betterment of the world that awaits your gifts. Let us therefore begin.

Commencement

O n this your final day at Lighthouse, I would like to say a few closing words. It is important that those of us who are here see things a bit differently from others. To begin with, we know that there is no magic to our methodology, our technology, our laboratories, or our library; that these are merely the tools for learning, not learning itself which can be acquired only through strong and consistent effort.

We also know that the process of education in these halls is arduous, that each year demands 1000 classes attended and an equal amount of time devoted to study outside of class, day in and day out.

We know, too, that the total of these 4000 lessons acquired over a period of four years in each subject, albeit important and enlightening, is no guarantee of entrance into the world's premier universities, no ticket to Harvard or Oxford.

But beyond this, I have two concerns. The first is that whatever success we may have gained in past years is no assurance of our continued success. Experience should ensure that our results improve every year, not simply remain the same. The difficult task is not so much in developing something new, but in maintaining the quality of what has already been developed. The real question is how good this school will be in the long run, how it may continue to develop and improve over time. Right now, its future and its reputation rests squarely in the hands of all who now sit in this room as well as those who shall be joining us hereafter.

My second concern is with the statements we often hear about getting well paid jobs. We have all heard parents talk about the necessity for getting a good education in order to get a good job. I understand the importance of gaining a comfortable living, but I want to take issue with this universal opinion about the role of jobs. I believe that the result of a good education far exceeds the mere necessity of working at some job.

Think of it this way. There is no job that awaits your joining it, no standard set of tasks to which you will automatically be prepared to undertake regardless of your education. For one thing, by the time you get ready to work, jobs in this city as well as elsewhere will already have changed, much as they have over the past four years—some old ones will have disappeared and some new ones come into play. And the ones still around will be busy adjusting to new methods and new circumstances because the world of work is never static. Today machines and computers do much of the work that individual employees used to do and this rate of change is bound to increase as time goes by. I doubt that there is an existing profession that will guarantee your satisfaction, for they, too, are under transformation. You are going to have to live by your wits just like your parents and grandparents have. Your life, in other words, is in your hands—not your parents or grandparents, not your teachers or your school, not the university you may attend.

Success in any job you undertake resides in your ability to alter the nature of that job, not merely to do what has already been done. The highest paid jobs are the ones only the few can do, not the ones anybody can do. Success is having other people pay you to do just what you want to do, what you would do without pay, not just what everybody else wants you to do or thinks is worth doing.

The mind you have is the only one you get, the one you are condemned to live with for the rest of your life. The purpose of education is to furnish that mind, to give it the power constantly to learn, to create, to change the way the world works. Perhaps in the course of your learning you have come to see how great ideas are initially met with heavy and prolonged resistance, how the world clings to the past and cowers from the future.

Life, it turns out, is not unlike learning that feeds upon change, that enforces alteration in what and how we think. To learn is to change, to discover, invent! Learning is the conquest of past illusions. We learn by experience because living requires adjustment. Do not listen to those who prate about the real world differing from the one you know. What is real is only what we have learned about the world and its ways, which is itself in a constant state of flux.

My advice is therefore to pray for something to do that will totally consume you, something that calls upon everything you know, that requires you to keep learning all your life, not just in school. For then you will be wise and people will come to you and ask what they should do in order to be happy. And your answer will be simple: do what you want to do just as I have done.